Voices That Shaped the Modern World

A Sourcebook 1500-Present

Edited by
Sarah L. Charton
University of Central Arkansas

KENDALL/HUNT PUBLISHING COMPANY
4050 Westmark Drive   Dubuque, Iowa 52002

Cover image copyright © 2006 JupiterImages Corporation

Copyright © 2006 by Kendall/Hunt Publishing Company

ISBN 13: 978-0-7575-3148-4
ISBN 10: 0-7575-3148-2

All rights reserved. No part of this publication may be reproduced, stored in a retrieval system, or transmitted, in any form or by any means, electronic, mechanical, photocopying, recording, or otherwise, without the prior written permission of the copyright owner.

Printed in the United States of America
10 9 8 7 6 5 4 3 2 1

Contents

Preface   *vii*

I. The Early Modern World, 1450–1815   *1*

European Expansion and the Acceleration of Global Contacts   *2*

Cortés and the Conquest of the Aztecs (1522)   *3*
A Native American Account of the Conquest (ca. 1528)   *6*
The Interesting Narrative of Olaudah Equiano (1789)   *8*
A View of the Ottoman Empire (1555–1562)   *13*
A Spanish Explorer's Description of the Pueblos (1580)   *16*
Leo Africanus's Descriptions of African Societies   *18*
The Chinese Emperor Addresses King George III of England (1793)   *21*

Absolutism & Constitutionalism   *23*

James I of England Speaks to Parliament (1610)   *24*
Duc de Saint-Simon, The Court of Louis XIV   *26*
Peter the Great: Westernizing Decrees (1701)   *29*
The English Bill of Rights (1689)   *32*
John Locke, *The Second Treatise of Government* (1690)   *37*

The Scientific Revolution & Enlightenment   *41*

Copernicus Gives His Reasons for Delaying Publication of *On the Revolutions* (1543)   *42*
Francis Bacon and the Method of Science (1620)   *44*
Voltaire, *A Treatise on Toleration* (1763)   *47*
Adam Smith's Free-Market Capitalism (1776)   *51*

The French Revolution   55

Declaration of the Rights of Man and of the Citizen (1789)   56
Declaration of the Rights of Woman and of the Citizen (1791)   59

II. The Long Nineteenth Century   63

The First Industrial Revolution in Europe   64

Charles Dickens, *Hard Times* (1854)   65
Testimony for the Factory Act of 1833: Working Conditions in England   67

Culture & Ideologies in Nineteenth Century Europe   71

Marx and Engels, *The Communist Manifesto* (1848)   72
Edmund Burke, *Reflections on the Revolution in France* (1790)   77
John Stuart Mill, "On Liberty" (1859)   80
Giuseppe Mazzini on Nationalism (1852)   83
Simón de Bolívar Addresses the Congress of Angostura (1819)   85
Theodor Herzl and Zionism (1896)   88
Charles Darwin, *The Descent of Man* (1871)   91

The New Imperialism   95

Jules Ferry Discusses French Colonialism (1884)   96
Europeans Carve Up the African "Cake" at Berlin (1885)   98
Rudyard Kipling, *The White Man's Burden* (1899)   100

III. The Modern World, 1900-1945   103

The First World War   104

Vladimir Il'ich Lenin, *What Is to Be Done?* (1902)   105
Woodrow Wilson, Speech on the Fourteen Points (1918)   108
The Treaty of Versailles (1919)   111

Dictatorship & the Second World War   115

The Program of the German Workers' Party (1920)   116
Adolf Hitler on "Nation and Race" (1925)   119
A. O. Avdienko Praises Stalin (1935)   125
Elie Wiesel, *Night*   127

IV. The Post-War World, 1945-Present *131*

The Cold War *132*

Winston Churchill's "Iron Curtain" Speech (1946) *133*
Containment (1946) *136*

Decolonization and Its Aftermath in the Non-Western World *141*

Gandhi on the Spinning Wheel and Satyagraha *142*
Vietnamese Declaration of Independence (1945) *145*
UN Declaration on Decolonization (1962) *148*
Julius Nyerere on One-Party Rule in Tanganyika (1961) *150*
José A. Silva Michelena, *The Illusion of Democracy in Dependent Nations* (1971) *153*
Genocide in Rwanda (1994) *159*
Osama bin Laden, "Hypocrisy Rears Its Ugly Head" (2001) *161*

The American Civil Rights Movement *163*

Martin Luther King Jr., Letter from Birmingham Jail (1963) *164*
Dwight D. Eisenhower, Events in Little Rock, Arkansas (1957) *167*

V. Map Exercises *171*

Preface

Voices That Shaped the Modern World, formerly known as *Landmarks of Modern World History*, is a collection of primary sources designed to supplement classroom lectures and textbook readings in world history classes. Primary sources are a vital link to the past, and their interpretation forms the basis of all solid historical inquiry, whether by a first-year undergraduate or an experienced historian. However, the basic intellectual skills that such work both develops and requires—analysis and synthesis, the ability to organize, summarize, compare, and critique information—are of use not only to the historian but right across the curriculum and, still more importantly, outside the university, in everyday life. This is true now more than ever as the internet and other new media give us access and exposure to ever greater amounts of information, not all of which is worth taking at face value.

With this in mind, the documents in this Reader—and the exercises accompanying them—have been designed specifically to improve and assess "critical thinking skills." The questions following each source have been designed not just to test reading comprehension, but also to encourage the student to dig a little deeper, to draw connections, make original inferences, and "read between the lines." They are exercises in historical detective work.

In some cases, this means that a question may reference an issue only indirectly dealt within the document itself. Thus, for example, the student is asked not only to locate and summarize Copernicus's reasons for delaying publication of his monumental 1543 work, *On the Revolutions* (p. 42), but also to make inferences—based on evidence in the text—about the intellectual environment in which Copernicus operated. Alternatively, students who read Leo Africanus's Descriptions of African Societies (p. 18), will be asked not only about the reading's explicit content but also to comb the section on "The City of Timbuktu" for indirect evidence about the city's political and social system. And so on. The point of such questions is *not* to send students scurrying to the library or internet to find more information about a given topic; nor is it to have them attempt to formulate conclusive or definitive historical answers; rather it is to help students draw out of the small piece of information contained in one document a reasonable, valid inference which they must then defend.

The book also encourages students to "get their hands dirty" while exercising their critical thinking faculties, for example by having them locate thesis statements or important content information, and by having them identify specific pieces of evidence relevant to a particular question, and so on. Since history happens in specific places as well as in time, map exercises have also been provided.

Students and faculty who are familiar with the original edition of this reader will notice a few changes in the format and content of the new one. For example, the organization of the reader has been improved in order to reflect more specific time periods in history, and new sources and maps have been provided as well. More importantly, the consumable nature of the reader has been abandoned in favor of a more traditional format, with critical thinking questions located at the end of each primary source for the convenience of the reader. It is my hope that these modifications will enhance the first-rate quality of the work already done by Dr. Bonhomme in the first edition.

Finally, I would like to acknowledge all of those people who were instrumental in the publication of the reader. First and foremost, I would like to thank the original editor, Brian Bonhomme, who was responsible for creating the first edition of the reader. Putting together a primary source reader from scratch is a monumental task, and his contributions should not be forgotten or overlooked. Other people who deserve recognition include the UCA world history faculty who provided much needed suggestions for improvements, especially Drs. Ken Barnes and Roger Pauly; the editorial staff at Kendall Hunt, in particular Stephen and Kimberly, who patiently guided me through the publication process; the secretaries of the department, Judy and Charlene; and my husband, Mac, as well as my parents, all of whom provided the moral support needed to accomplish this task.

Sarah L. Charton
University of Central Arkansas

I. The Early Modern World, 1450-1815

European Expansion and the Acceleration of Global Contacts

Cortés and the Conquest of the Aztecs (1522)

A Native American Account of the Conquest (ca. 1528)

The Interesting Narrative of Olaudah Equiano (1789)

A View of the Ottoman Empire (1555-1562)

A Spanish Explorer's Description of the Pueblos (1580)

Leo Africanus's Descriptions of African Societies

The Chinese Emperor Addresses King George III of England (1793)

Cortés and the Conquest of the Aztecs

(1522)

The fall of Tenochtitlán made possible the eventual Spanish conquest and domination of much of South America in general. Here, Cortés describes the event in letters to the Spanish monarch, Charles V.

The next day, those chiefs came to our camp very early in the morning and asked me to come to the square of the market of the city, because their sovereign wished to speak to me. Believing it was true, I mounted my horse and awaited him where it had been agreed, for more than three or four hours, but he never chose to appear before me. As I saw the mockery, and it had already become late, and that neither the other messengers nor the lord came, I sent for the Indians, our friends, who had been left at the entrance of the city almost a league from where we were, whom I had ordered not to advance beyond there because the people of the city had asked me that, whilst treating for peace none of them should be inside it. Neither they nor those of Pedro de Alvarado's camp delayed in coming, and, when they arrived, we attacked some of the barricades and water streets which they held, no other strong force being left them, and we charged amongst them ourselves, as well as our friends, according as we pleased. Before leaving the camp, I had ordered that Gonzalo de Sandoval should proceed with the brigantines to the place where the Indians had fortified themselves in the houses, thus holding them surrounded, but not attacking them until he should observe that we began to fight; in such manner that, holding them thus surrounded, they had no place to go except amongst the dead, and on the roofs which were left them. For this cause, they neither had, nor procured, arrows, nor darts, nor stones, with which to hurt us. Our friends accompanied us, armed with swords and shields, and such was the slaughter done that day on water and on land, that with prisoners taken they numbered in all more than forty thousand men; and such were the shrieks and the weeping of the women and children that there was none whose heart did not break; and we had more trouble in preventing our allies from killing and inflicting tortures than we had in fighting with the Indians, for no such inhuman cruelty as the natives of these parts practice was ever seen amongst any people. Our allies obtained very great plunder, which we could not prevent, because we were about nine hundred Spaniards, and they more than one hundred and fifty thousand men, and no attention or diligence was sufficient to prevent them from robbing, although we did everything possible to stop it. One of the reasons why I refused to go to extremes in those previous days was that, by taking them by assault, they would probably throw what they had into the lake, and if they did not do so our allies would steal everything they found; and, for this reason, I feared that but a small part of the great wealth existing in the city, as shown by what I had before obtained for Your Highness, would be

---

From *Fernando Cortes, His Five Letters of Relation to the Emperror Charles V*, translated by F.A. MacNutt, 1908.

secured for Your Majesty. As it was already late, and we could no longer endure the stench of the dead which had lain for many days in those streets (the most pestilential thing in the world), we returned to our camps.

That afternoon, I arranged that, as on the next day following we should again enter the city, three large field pieces should be prepared which we would take to the city, because, as I feared that the enemy were so compact that they could not turn round, the Spaniards in charging might be crushed by mere numbers, and therefore I wanted to do them some damage with the field pieces in order to force them out towards us. I ordered the alguacil mayor likewise to be prepared to enter, the next day, with the brigantines, through the canals of a large lake extending amongst some houses where the canoes of the city were all gathered; and there were already so few houses left where they might shelter that the lord of the city, with certain of the chiefs, had placed himself in a canoe, not knowing what to do with themselves. Thus we planned our entrance on the morning of the following day.

When day had dawned, I had our whole force prepared, and the large field pieces brought out; and I had, the day before, ordered Pedro de Alvarado to await me in the square of the market-place, and not to begin fighting until I arrived. All being assembled, and the brigantines ready for action, behind the houses on the water, where the enemy were gathered, I ordered that, on hearing a musket-shot, the land force should enter the small part which was still to be captured, and force the enemy towards the water where the brigantines would be awaiting them; and I cautioned them particularly to look after Quatamucin, and to endeavor to take him alive, because then the war would stop. I mounted the top of a roof, and, before the fight began, I spoke with some of the chiefs of the city whom I knew, and asked them why their lord did not come, seeing that they were in such straits, and I said they ought not to be the cause of all perishing; and told them to call him, saying that nobody need be afraid; and it seemed that two of those chiefs went to call him. After a short time, they returned with one of the highest chiefs of all of them, who was called Ciguacoacin, captain and governor of them all, whose counsel was followed in everything concerning the war. I showed a very good disposition towards him, so that he might be reassured and have no fears and finally he told me that the sovereign would in no way appear before me, and that he rather preferred to die where he was, and that he himself was much grieved at this decision but that I could do as I pleased. Recognising by this his determination, I told him to return to his own people, and that he and they might prepare themselves, as I was determined to attack them, and finish destroying them; and so it happened. More than five hours had passed in these parleyings, and the inhabitants of the city were all treading on the dead, others in the water were swimming, and others drowning themselves in the large lake where the canoes were collected. Such was the plight in which they were, that no understanding could conceive how they could endure it; and an infinite number of men, women, and children kept coming towards us, who, in their haste, pushed one another back into the water and were drowned amidst the multitude of dead. It appears they had perished to the number of more than fifty thousand, from the salt water which they drank, or from starvation, and pestilence. All these bodies, (in order that we should not understand their extremity), were neither thrown into the water lest the brigantines might come across them, nor were they thrown outside their boundary, lest we should see them about the city; and thus, in the streets they occupied, were found heaps of dead, so that nobody could step without trampling them. As the people of the city came towards us, I ordered Spaniards to be stationed in all the streets, to prevent our allies from killing those unhappy creatures, who were beyond number; and I also ordered the captains of our allies not to allow in any way those fugitives to be killed, but, as they were so many, it was not possible to prevent it that day, so more than fifteen thousand persons were massacred. Meanwhile, some of the chiefs and warriors of the city were brought to bay on some roofs and in the water, where they could no longer stop, or hide from all their disasters and their weakness which had become very apparent; and, seeing that the afternoon was coming on us, and that they would not surrender, I had two large field pieces directed against them to see whether they would surrender then, because they would suffer greater damage by our giving permission to our friends to attack them, than by those two field pieces, which caused some destruction. As this also brought no result, I ordered the signal of the musket to be fired, whereupon the corner they still held was immediately taken, and those who were in it forced into the water, and others who had not fought surrendered. The brigantines swiftly entered that lake, and broke into the midst of the fleet of canoes, and the warriors no longer ventured to fight.

It pleased God that the captain of a brigantine, called Garci Holguin, overtook a canoe in which there were some distinguished people, and, as he had two or three cross-bowmen in the prow of the brigantine, and was crossing in the front of the canoe, they signaled to him not to shoot because their sovereign was there. The canoe was quickly captured, and they took Quatamucin, and the lord of Tacuba, and the other chiefs who were with him; and the said captain, Garci Holguin, immediately brought the said sovereign of the city and the other chief prisoners to the terrace where I was, which was near the lake. When I invited them to sit down, not wishing to show any rigor, he approached me and said to me in his language that he had done all that on his part he was bound to do to defend himself and his people, until he was reduced to that state, and that I might now do with him as I chose; and placing his hand on a dagger which I wore he bade me stab him with it and kill him. I encouraged him, and told him not to be afraid; and this lord having been made prisoner, the war immediately ceased, which God Our Lord was pleased to bring to its end on this day, the Feast of San Hipolito, which was the 13th of August in the year 1521. So that from the day when we laid the siege to the city, which was the 30th of May of the said year, until it was taken, seventy-five days passed, in which Your Majesty may perceive the hardships, dangers, and cruelties, which these, your vassals, suffered, and in which they so exposed themselves that their deeds will bear testimony of them. In all these seventy-five days of the siege, none passed without more or less fighting.

Critical Thinking Questions

1. What can you infer from the reading about Cortés's opinions about the Americans he was fighting?

2. How does Cortés portray his actions toward the Americans? What can you infer about his opinion about Spain and his own cause?

3. What can you infer from the reading about Cortés's personality?

A Native American Account of the Conquest
(ca. 1528)

The following is a narration of the later stages of the Spanish siege of Tenochtitlán. It comes from Tlatelolco, a Native American community bordering Tenochtitlán in the north. "Cuauhtemoc" is an alternative rendering of the Aztec leader's name, given in the previous document as Quatamucin. The term "3-House" is the Native American designation for the year 1519.

Now the Spaniards began to wage war against us. They attacked us by land for ten days, and then their ships appeared. Twenty days later, they gathered all their ships together near Nonohualco, off the place called Mazatzintamalco. The allies from Tlaxcala and Huexotzinco set up camp on either side of the road.

Our warriors from Tlatelolco immediately leaped into their canoes and set out for Mazatzintamalco and the Nonohualco road. But no one set out from Tenochtitlan to assist us: only the Tlatelolcas were ready when the Spaniards arrived in their ships. On the following day, the ships sailed to Xoloco.

The fighting at Xoloco and Huitzillan lasted for two days. While the battle was under way, the warriors from Tenochtitlan began to mutiny. They said: "Where are our chiefs? They have fired scarcely a single arrow! Do they think they have fought like men?" Then they seized four of their own leaders and put them to death. The victims were two captains, Cuauhnochtli and Cuapan, and the priests of Amantlan and Tlalocan. This was the second time that the people of Tenochtitlan killed their own leaders.

The Spaniards set up two cannons in the middle of the road and aimed them at the city. When they fired them, one of the shots struck the Eagle Gate. The people of the city were so terrified that they began to flee to Tlatelolco. They brought their idol Huitzilopochtli with them, setting it up in the House of the Young Men. Their king Cuauhtemoc also abandoned Tenochtitlan. Their chiefs said: "Mexicanos! Tlatelolcas! All is not lost! We can still defend our houses. We can prevent them from capturing our storehouses and the produce of our lands. We can save the sustenance of life, our stores of còrn. We can also save our weapons and insignia, our clusters of rich feathers, our gold earrings and precious stones. Do not be discouraged; do not lose heart. We are Mexicanos! We are Tlatelolcas!"

During the whole time we were fighting, the warriors of Tenochtitlan were nowhere to be seen. The battles of Yacacolco, Atezcapan, Coatlan, Nonohualco, Xoxohuitlan, Tepeyacac and elsewhere were all fought by ourselves, by Tlatelolcas. In the same way, the canals were defended solely by Tlatelolcas.

The captains from Tenochtitlan cut their hair short, and so did those of lesser rank. The Otomies

---

From *The Broken Spears: Aztec Account of the Conquest* by Miquel Leon-Portilla, 1962.

and the other ranks that usually wore headdresses did not wear them during all the time we were fighting. The Tlatelolcas surrounded the most important captains and their women taunted them: "Why are you hanging back? Have you no shame? No woman will ever paint her face for you again!" The wives of the men from Tenochtitlan wept and begged for pity.

When the warriors of Tlatelolco heard what was happening, they began to shout, but still the brave captains of Tenochtitlan hung back. As for the Tlatelolcas, their humblest warriors died fighting as bravely as their captains....

The Spaniards made ready to attack us, and the war broke out again. They assembled their forces in Cuepopan and Cozcacuahco. A vast number of our warriors were killed by their metal darts. Their ships sailed to Texopan, and the battle there lasted three days. When they had forced us to retreat, they entered the Sacred Patio, where there was a four-day battle. Then they reached Yacacolco.

The Tlatelolcas set up three racks of heads in three different places. The first rack was in the Sacred Patio of Tlilancalco [Black House], where we strung up the heads of our lords the Spaniards. The second was in Acacolco, where we strung up Spanish heads and the heads of two of their horses. The third was in Zacatla, in front of the temple of the earth-goddess Cihuacoatl, where we strung up the heads of Tlaxcaltecas.

The women of Tlatelolco joined in the fighting. They struck at the enemy and shot arrows at them; they tucked up their skirts and dressed in the regalia of war.

The Spaniards forced us to retreat. Then they occupied the market place. The Tlatelolcas—the Jaguar Knights, the Eagle Knights, the great warriors—were defeated, and this was the end of the battle. It had lasted five days, and two thousand Tlatelolcas were killed in action. During the battle, the Spaniards set up a canopy for the Captain in the market place. They also mounted a catapult on the temple platform....

Cuauhtemoc was taken to Cortes along with three other princes. The Captain was accompanied by Pedro de Alvarado and La Malinche.

When the princes were made captives, the people began to leave, searching for a place to stay. Everyone was in tatters, and the women's thighs were almost naked. The Christians searched all the refugees. They even opened the women's skirts and blouses and felt everywhere: their ears, their breasts, their hair. Our people scattered in all directions. They went to neighboring villages and huddled in corners in the houses of strangers.

The city was conquered in the year 3-House. The date on which we departed was the day 1-Serpent in the ninth month.

Critical Thinking Questions

1. Briefly comment on any parts of the text that seem to offer a different interpretation of events or otherwise notably contrast with Cortés's account of the conquest.

2. What can you infer from the document regarding the opinion the Tlatelolcas (who wrote the document) had of their southern neighbors the "warriors from Tenochtitlán"?

The Interesting Narrative of Olaudah Equiano
(1789)

Olaudah Equiano, an Ibo, was born in 1745 in what is now Nigeria. As a young boy he was captured by African slavers and later sold to European slave traders who transported him to the West Indies. Unlike most slaves, he received a Western education and was eventually able to purchase his freedom. His efforts to help achieve the abolition of the slave trade led him to write his autobiography, from which the following is excerpted.

I hope the reader will not think I have trespassed on his patience in introducing myself to him with some account of the manners and customs of my country. They had been implanted in me with great care, and made an impression on my mind, which time could not erase, and which all the adversity and variety of fortune I have since experienced served only to rivet and record; for, whether the love of one's country be real or imaginary, or a lesson of reason, or an instinct of nature, I still look back with pleasure on the first scenes my life, though that pleasure has been for the most part mingled with sorrow.

I have already acquainted the reader with the time and place of my birth. My father, besides many slaves, had a numerous family, of which seven lived to grow up, including myself and a sister, who was the only daughter. As I was the youngest of the sons, I became, of course, the greatest favourite with my mother, and was always with her; and she used to take particular pains to form my mind. I was trained up from my earliest years in the arts of agriculture and war: my daily exercise was shooting and throwing javelins; and my mother adorned me with emblems, after the manner of our greatest warriors. In this way I grew up till I was turned the age of eleven, when an end was put to my happiness in the following manner:—Generally, when the grown people in the neighbourhood were gone far in the fields to labour, the children assembled together in some of the neighbour's premises to play; and commonly some of us used to get up a tree to look out for any assailant, or kidnapper, that might come upon us; for they sometimes took those opportunities of our parents' absence, to attack and carry off as many as they could seize. One day, as I was watching at the top of a tree in our yard, I saw one of those people come into the yard of our next neighbour but one, to kidnap, there being many stout young people in it. Immediately, on this, I gave the alarm of the rogue, and he was surrounded by the stoutest of them, who entangled him with cords, so that he could not escape till some of the grown people came and secured him. But alas! ere long, it was my fate to be thus attacked, and to be carried off, when none of the grown people were nigh. One day, when all our people were gone out to their works as usual, and only I and my dear sister were left to mind the

---

From *The Interesting Narrative of Olaudah Equiano*, London, 1789.

house, two men and a woman got over our walls, and in a moment seized us both; and, without giving us time to cry out, or make resistance, they stopped our mouths, and ran off with us into the nearest wood. Here they tied our hands, and continued to carry us as far as they could, till night came on, when we reached a small house, where the robbers halted for refreshment, and spent the night. We were then unbound; but were unable to take any food; and, being quite overpowered by fatigue and grief, our only relief was some sleep, which allayed our misfortune for a short time. The next morning we left the house, and continued travelling all the day. For a long time we had kept the woods, but at last we came into a road which I believed I knew. I had now some hopes of being delivered; for we had advanced but a little way before I discovered some people at a distance, on which I began to cry out for their assistance; but my cries had no other effect than to make them tie me faster and stop my mouth, and then they put me into a large sack. They also stopped my sister's mouth, and tied her hands; and in this manner we proceeded till we were out of the sight of these people. When we went to rest the following night they offered us some victuals; but we refused them; and the only comfort we had was in being in one another's arms all that night, and bathing each other with our tears. But alas! we were soon deprived of even the smallest comfort of weeping together. The next day proved a day of greater sorrow than I had yet experienced; for my sister and I were then separated, while we lay clasped in each other's arms: it was in vain that we besought them not to part us: she was torn from me, and immediately carried away, while I was left in a state of distraction not to be described. I cried and grieved continually; and for several days did not eat any thing but what they forced into my mouth. At length, after many days travelling, during which I had often changed masters, I got into the hands of a chieftain, in a very pleasant country. This man had two wives and some children, and they all used me extremely well, and did all they could to comfort me; particularly the first wife, who was something like my mother. Although I was a great many days journey from my father's house, yet these people spoke exactly the same language with us. This first master of mine, as I may call him, was a smith; and my principal employment was working his bellows, which were the same kind as I had seen in my vicinity. They were in some respects not unlike the stoves here in gentlemen's kitchens; and were covered over with leather; and in the middle of that leather a stick was fixed, and a person stood up, and worked it, in the same manner as is done to pump water out of a cask with a hand pump. I believe it was gold he worked, for it was of a lovely bright yellow colour, and was worn by the women on their wrists and ancles. I was there I suppose about a month, and they at least used to trust me some little distance from the house. This liberty I used in embracing every opportunity to inquire the way to my own home: and I also sometimes, for the same purpose, went with the maidens, in the cool of the evenings, to bring pitchers of water from the springs for the use of the house. I had also remarked where the sun rose in the morning, and set in the evening, as I had travelled along; and I had observed that my father's house was towards the rising of the sun. I therefore determined to seize the first opportunity of making my escape, and to shape my course for that quarter; for I was quite oppressed and weighed down by grief after my mother and friends; and my love of liberty, ever great, was strengthened by the mortifying circumstance of not daring to eat with the free-born children, although I was mostly their companion. While I was projecting my escape one day, an unlucky event happened, which quite disconcerted my plan, and put an end to my hopes. I used to be sometimes employed in assisting an elderly woman slave to cook and take care of the poultry; and one morning, while I was feeding some chickens, I happened to toss a small pebble at one of them, which hit it on the middle, and directly killed it. The old slave, having soon after missed the chicken, inquired after it; and on my relating the accident (for I told her the truth, because my mother would never suffer me to tell a lie), she flew into a violent passion, threatening that I should suffer for it; and, my master being out, she immediately went and told her mistress what I had done. This alarmed me very much, and I expected an instant flogging, which to me was uncommonly dreadful; for I had seldom been beaten at home. I therefore resolved to fly; and accordingly I ran into a thicket that was hard by, and hid myself in the bushes.... The neighbours continued the whole day looking for me, ... but they never discovered me,... [Equiano, driven by hunger and fear of attack, returns to the household from which he had run.] [I] crept to my master's kitchen, from whence I set out at first, and which was an open shed, and laid myself down in the ashes with an anxious wish for death to relieve me from all my pains. I was scarcely awake in the morning, when the old woman slave who was the first up, came to light the fire, and saw me in the fire place. . . . She now promised to intercede for me, and went for her master, who soon after came, and, having slightly reprimanded me, ordered me to be taken care of, and not ill-treated.

Soon after this my master's only daughter and child by his first wife sickened and died, which affected him so much that for some time he was almost frantic, and really would have killed himself, had he not been watched and prevented. However, in a small time afterwards he recovered; and I was again sold. I was now carried to the left of the sun's rising, through many dreary wastes and dismal woods, amidst the hideous roarings of wild beasts. The people I was sold to used to carry me very often, when I was tired, either on their shoulders or on their backs. I saw many convenient well-built sheds along the roads, at proper distances, to accommodate the merchants and travellers, who lay in those buildings along with their wives, who often accompany them; and they always go well armed.

From the time I left my own nation I always found somebody that understood me till I came to the sea coast. The languages of different nations did not totally differ, nor were they so copious as those of the Europeans, particularly the English. They were therefore easily learned; and, while I was journeying thus through Africa, I acquired two or three different tongues. In this manner I had been travelling for a considerable time, when one evening, to my great surprise, whom should I see brought to the house where I was but my dear sister? As soon as she saw me she gave a loud shriek, and ran into my arms—I was quite overpowered: neither of us could speak, but, for a considerable time, clung to each other in mutual embraces, unable to do any thing but weep. Our meeting affected all who saw us; and indeed I must acknowledge, in honour of those sable destroyers of human rights, that I never met with any ill treatment, or saw any offered to their slaves, except tying them, when necessary, to keep them from running away. When these people knew we were brother and sister, they indulged us to be together; and the man, to whom I supposed we belonged, lay with us, he in the middle, while she and I held one another by the hands across his breast all night; and thus for a while we forgot our misfortunes in the joy of being together; but even this small comfort was soon to have an end; for scarcely had the fatal morning appeared, when she was again torn from me forever! I was now more miserable, if possible, than before. . . .

I did not long remain after my sister. I was again sold, and carried through a number of places, till, after travelling a considerable time, I came to a town called Timnah, in the most beautiful country I had yet seen in Africa. . . . I was sold here for one hundred and seventy-two [cowrie shells] by a merchant who lived and brought me there. I had been about two or three days at his house, when a wealthy widow, a neighbour of his, came there one evening, and brought with her an only son, a young gentleman about my own age and size. Here they saw me; and, having taken a fancy to me, I was bought of the merchant, and went home with them. Her house and premises were situated close to one of those rivulets I have mentioned, and were the finest I ever saw in Africa: they were very extensive, and she had a number of slaves to attend her. The next day I was washed and perfumed, and when mealtime came, I was led into the presence of my mistress, and eat and drank before her with her son. This filled me with astonishment; and I could scarce help expressing my surprise that the young gentleman should suffer me, who was bound, to eat with him who was free; and not only so, but that he would not at any time either eat or drink till I had taken first, because I was the eldest, which was agreeable to our custom. Indeed every thing here, and all their treatment of me, made me forget that I was a slave. The language of these people resembled ours so nearly, that we understood each other perfectly. They had also the very same customs as we. There were likewise slaves daily to attend us. . . . In this resemblance to my former happy state, I passed about two months, and I now began to think I was to be adopted into the family, and was beginning to be reconciled to my situation, and to forget by degrees my misfortunes, when all at once the delusion vanished; for, without the least previous knowledge, one morning early, while my dear master and companion was still asleep, I was awakened out of my reverie to fresh sorrow, and hurried away. . . .

Thus, at the very moment I dreamed of the greatest happiness, I found myself most miserable; and it seemed as if fortune wished to give me this taste of joy only to render the reverse more poignant. The change I now experienced was as painful as it was sudden and unexpected. It was a change indeed from a state of bliss to a scene which is inexpressible by me, as it discovered to me an element I had never before beheld, and till then had no idea of, and wherein such instances of hardship and fatigue continually occurred as I can never reflect on but with horror.

All the nations and people I had hitherto passed through resembled our own in their manners, customs, and language; but I came at length to a country, the inhabitants of which differed from us in all those particulars. I was very much struck with this difference, especially when I came among a people who did not circumcise, and eat without washing their hands. They cooked also in iron pots, and had European cutlasses and cross bows, which were unknown to us, and fought with their fists among themselves. Their women were not so modest as ours, for they eat, and drank, and slept with their men. But, above all, I was amazed to see no sacrifices or offerings among them. In some of those places the people ornamented themselves with scars, and likewise filed their teeth very sharp. They wanted sometimes to ornament me in the same manner, but I would not suffer them; hoping that I might some time be among a people who did not thus disfigure themselves, as I thought they did. At last, I came to the banks of a large river, which was covered with canoes, in which the people appeared to live with their household utensils and provisions of all kinds. I was beyond measure astonished at this, as I had never before seen any water larger than a pond or a rivulet; and my surprise was mingled with no small fear, when I was put into one of these canoes, and we began to paddle and move along the river. We continued going on thus till night; and, when we came to land, and made fires on the banks, each family by themselves, some dragged their canoes on shore, others stayed and cooked in theirs, and lay in them all night. Those on the land had mats, of which they made tents, some in the shape of little houses: In these we slept; and, after the morning meal, we embarked again, and proceeded as before. I was often very much astonished to see some of the women, as well as the men, jump into the water, dive to the bottom, come up again, and swim about. Thus I continued to travel, sometimes by land, sometimes by water, through different countries, and various nations, till, at the end of six or seven months after I had been kidnapped I arrived at the sea-coast....

The first object which saluted my eyes when I arrived on the coast was the sea, and a slaveship, which was then riding at anchor, and waiting for its cargo. These filled me with astonishment, which was soon converted into terror, which I am yet at a loss to describe, nor the then feelings of my mind. When I was carried on board I was immediately handled, and tossed up, to see if I were sound, by some of the crew; and I was now persuaded that I had got into a world of bad spirits, and that they were going to kill me. Their complexions too differing so much from ours, their long hair, and the language they spoke, which was very different from any I had ever heard, united to confirm me in this belief. Indeed, such were the horrors of my views and fears at the moment, that, if ten thousand worlds had been my own, I would have freely parted with them all to have exchanged my condition with that of the meanest slave in my own country. When I looked round the ship too, and saw a large furnace or copper boiling, and a multitude of black people of every description chained together, every one of their countenances expressing dejection and sorrow, I no longer doubted of my fate; and, quite overpowered with horror and anguish, I fell motionless on the deck and fainted. When I recovered a little, I found some black people about me, who I believed were some of those who brought me on board, and had been receiving their pay; they talked to me in order to cheer me, but all in vain. I asked them if we were not to be eaten by those white men with horrible looks, red faces, and long hair. They told me I was not; and one of the crew brought me a small portion of spirituous liquor in a wine-glass; but, being afraid of him, I would not take it out of his hand. One of the blacks therefore took it from him, and gave it to me, and I took a little down my palate, which, instead of reviving me, as they thought it would, threw me into the greatest consternation at the strange feeling it produced having never tasted any such liquor before. Soon after this, the blacks who brought me on board went off, and left me abandoned to despair. I now saw myself deprived of all chance of returning to my native country, or even the least glimpse of hope of gaining the shore, which I now considered as friendly; and I even wished for my former slavery, in preference to my present situation, which was filled with horrors of every kind, still heightened by my ignorance of what I was to undergo. I was not long suffered to indulge my grief; I was soon put down under the decks, and there I received such a salutation in my nostrils as I had never experienced in my life; so that, with the loathsomeness of the stench, and crying together, I became so sick and low that I was not able to eat, nor had I the least desire to taste any thing. I now wished for the last friend, death, to relieve me; but soon, to my grief, two of the white men offered me eatables; and, on my refusing to eat, one of them held me fast by the hands, and laid me across, I think, the windlass, and tied my feet while the other flogged me severely. I had never experienced any thing of this kind before; and, although not being used to the water, I naturally feared that element the first time I saw it; yet, nevertheless, could I have got over the nettings, I would have jumped over the side; but I could not; and, besides, the crew used to watch us very closely who were not chained down to the decks, lest we should leap into the water: and I have seen some of these poor African prisoners most severely cut for attempting to do so, and hourly whipped for not eating. This indeed was often the case with myself. In a little time after, amongst the poor chained men, I found some of my own nation, which in a small degree gave ease to my mind. I inquired of them what was to be done with us? They gave me to understand we were to be carried to these white people's country to work for them.

Critical Thinking Questions

1. Early in the previous account, Equiano tells how he accidentally killed a chicken and then fled from the household of his "first master . . ., a smith." What can you infer here about his life in this household? Was he relatively well treated or not, for example?

2. How does Equiano view the Europeans when he first sees them? Why?

3. How was Equiano treated by the European or white traders he encountered on the ship (near the end of his account)? How was this different from his experience as a slave while still in Africa?

A View of the Ottoman Empire
(1555-1562)

The following comes from a series of letters written by Ogier Ghiselin de Busbecq, Holy Roman ambassador to Constantinople. The letters provide important descriptions of Ottoman (Turkish) government, military, customs, etc.

First Impressions

On our arrival . . . we were taken to call on Achmet Pasha (the chief Vizier) and the other pashas—for the Sultan himself was not then in the town—and commenced our negotiations with them touching the business entrusted to us by King Ferdinand. The pashas . . . told us that the whole matter depended on the Sultan's pleasure. On his arrival we were admitted to an audience; but the manner and spirit in which he . . . listened to our address, our arguments, and our message was by no means favorable. . . .

On entering we were separately conducted into the royal presence by the chamberlains, who grasped our arms. . . . After having gone through a pretense of kissing his hand, we were conducted backwards to the wall opposite his seat, care being taken that we should never turn our backs on him. The Sultan then listened to what I had to say; but the language I used was not at all to his taste, for the demands of his Majesty breathed a spirit of independence and dignity, which was by no means acceptable to one who deemed that his wish was law; and so he made no answer beyond saying in an impatient way, "Giusel, giusel," i.e. well, well. After this we were dismissed to our quarters.

The Sultan's hall was crowded with people, among whom were several officers of high rank. Besides these there were all the troopers of the Imperial guard, and a large force of Janissaries, but there was not in all that great assembly a single man who owed his position to anything save his valor and his merit. No distinction is attached to birth among the Turks; the respect to be paid to a man is measured by the position he holds in the public service. There is no fighting for precedence; a man's place is marked out by the duties he discharges. . . . It is by merit that men rise in the service, a system which ensures that posts should only be assigned to the competent. . . . Those who receive the highest offices from the Sultan are for the most part the sons of shepherds or herdsmen, and so far from being ashamed of their parentage, they actually glory in it, and consider it a matter of boasting that they owe nothing to the accident of birth; for they do not believe that high qualities are either natural or hereditary, nor do they think that they can be handed down from father to son, but that they are partly the gift of God, and partly the result of good training, great industry, and unwearied zeal. . . . Among the Turks, therefore, honors, high posts, and judgeships are the rewards of great ability and good service.

Ottoman Military Strength

Against us stands Suleiman, that foe whom his own and his ancestors' exploits have made so terrible; he tramples the soil of Hungary with 200,000 horse, he is at the very gates of Austria, threatens the rest of Germany, and brings in his train all the nations that extend from our borders to those of

---

From *The Life and Letters of Ogier Ghiselin De Burbecq*, London: Kegan Paul, 1881.

Persia. The army he leads is equipped with the wealth of many kingdoms. Of the three regions, into which the world is divided, there is not one that does not contribute its share towards our destruction....

The Turkish monarch going to war takes with him over 40,000 camels and nearly as many baggage mules, of which a great part, when he is invading Persia, are loaded with rice and other kinds of grain. These mules and camels also serve to carry tents and armor, and likewise tools and munitions for the campaign. The territories, which bear the name of Persia, ... are less fertile than our country, and even such crops as they bear are laid waste by the inhabitants in time of invasion in hopes of starving out the enemy, so that it is very dangerous for an army to invade Persia, if it is not furnished with abundant supplies.

The invading army carefully abstains from encroaching on its magazines at the outset; as they are well aware that, when the season for campaigning draws to a close, they will have to retreat over districts wasted by the enemy, or scraped as bare by countless hordes of men and droves of baggage animals, as if they had been devastated by locusts; accordingly they reserve their stores as much as possible for this emergency. Then the Sultan's magazines are opened, and a ration just sufficient to sustain life is daily weighed out to the Janissaries and other troops of the royal household. The rest of the army are badly off, unless they have provided some supplies at their own expense. And this is generally the case, for the greater number, and especially the cavalry, having from their long experience in war already felt such inconveniences, lead with them a pack horse, ... on which they carry many of the necessaries of life; namely, a small piece of canvas which they use as a tent, ... with the addition of some clothes and bedding; and as provisions for their private use, a leather bag or two of the finest flour, with a small pot of butter, and some spices and salt, on which they sustain life when they are hard pressed.... In this way they are able to support themselves from their own supplies for a month, or if necessary longer....

Family Life

The Turks are the most careful people in the world of the modesty of their wives, and therefore keep them shut up at home and hide them away, so that they scarce see the light of day. But if they have to go into the streets, they are sent out so covered and wrapped up in veils that they seem to those who meet them mere gliding ghosts. They have the means of seeing men through their linen or silken veils, while no part of their own body is exposed to men's view. For it is a received opinion among them, that no woman who is distinguished in the very smallest degree by her figure or youth can be seen by a man without his desiring her, and therefore without her receiving some contamination; and so it is the universal practice to confine the women to the harem. Their brothers are allowed to see them, but not their brothers-in-law. Men of the richer classes, or of higher rank, make it a condition when they marry, that their wives shall never set foot outside the threshold, and that no man or woman shall be admitted to see them for any reason whatever, not even their nearest relations, except their fathers and mothers, who are allowed to pay a visit to their daughters at the Turkish Easter.

On the other hand, if the wife has a father of high rank, or has brought a larger dowry than usual, the husband promises on his part that he will take no concubine, but will keep to her alone. Otherwise, the Turks are not forbidden by any law to have as many concubines as they please in addition to their lawful wives. Between the children of wives and those of concubines there is no distinction, and they are considered to have equal rights. As for concubines they either buy them for themselves or win them in war; when they are tired of them there is nothing to prevent their bringing them to market and selling them; but they are entitled to their freedom if they have borne children to their master.... A wife who has a portion settled on her is mistress of her husband's house, and all the other women have to obey her orders. The husband, however, may choose which of them shall spend the night with him. He makes known his wishes to the wife, and she sends to him the slave he has selected.... Only Friday night, which is their Sabbath, is supposed to belong to the wife; and she grumbles if her husband deprives her of it. On all the other nights he may do so as he pleases.

Divorces are granted among them for many reasons which it is easy for the husbands to invent. The divorced wife receives back her dowry, unless the divorce has been caused by some fault on her part. There is more difficulty in a woman's getting a divorce from her husband.

Critical Thinking Questions

1. What kind of government can we infer existed within the Ottoman Empire?

2. According to the document, how do officers and others in the Ottoman court get their power and position?

3. What can be learned from the document about the condition of Ottoman women at the time? Did women have any legal rights or protections?

A Spanish Explorer's Description of the Pueblos
(1580)

"Pueblos" are groupings of flat-roofed adobe or stone dwellings built by Southwestern Native Americans. The term is also used to identify the Natives themselves. The following description of Pueblo life highlights many of the complexities of this unique culture.

The people sustain themselves on corn, beans, and calabashes. They make tortillas and corn-flour gruel *(atole),* have buffalo meat and turkeys—they have large numbers of the latter. There is not an Indian who does not have a corral for his turkeys, each of which holds a flock of one hundred birds. The natives wear Campeche-type cotton blankets, for they have large cotton fields. They raise many small shaggy dogs—which, however, are not like those owned by the Spaniards—and build underground huts in which they keep these animals. . . .

After we took our leave of this people, the Indians led us to a large pueblo of another nation, where the inhabitants received us by making the sign of the cross with their hands in token of peace, as the others had done before. As the news spread, the procedure in this pueblo was followed in the others.

We entered the settlement, where the inhabitants gave us much corn. They showed us many ollas and other earthenware containers, richly painted, and brought quantities of calabashes and beans for us to eat. We took a little, so that they should not think we were greedy nor yet receive the impression that we did not want it; among themselves they consider it disparaging if one does not accept what is offered. One must take what they give, but after taking it may throw it away wherever he wishes. Should one throw it to the ground, they will not pick it up, though it may be something they can utilize. On the contrary, they will sooner let the thing rot where it is discarded. This is their practice. Thus, since we understood their custom, we took something of what they gave us. Moreover, we did this to get them into the habit of giving freely without being asked. Accordingly, they all brought what they could. The supply of corn tortillas, corn-flour gruel, calabashes, and beans which they brought was such that enough was left over every day to feed five hundred men. Part of this the natives carried for us. The women make tortillas similar to those of New Spain, and tortillas of ground beans, too. In these pueblos there are also houses of three and four stories, similar to the ones we had seen before; but the farther one goes into the interior the larger are the pueblos and the houses, and the more numerous the people.

The way they build their houses, which are in blocks, is as follows: they burn the clay, build narrow walls, and make abodes for the doorways. The

---

From *The Rediscovery of New Mexico: 1580–1594* by George Peter Hammond. Reprinted by permission of University of New Mexico Press.

lumber used is pine or willow; and many rounded beams, ten and twelve feet long, are built into the houses. The natives have ladders by means of which they climb to their quarters. These are movable wooden ladders, for when the Indians retire at night, they pull them up to protect themselves against enemies since they are at war with one another.

These people are handsome and fair-skinned. They are very industrious. Only the men attend to the work in the cornfields. The day hardly breaks before they go about with hoes in their hands. The women busy themselves only in the preparation of food, and in making and painting their pottery and *chicubites,* in which they prepare their bread. These vessels are so excellent and delicate that the process of manufacture is worth watching; for they equal, and even surpass, the pottery made in Portugal. The women also make earthen jars for carrying and storing water. These are very large, and are covered with lids of the same material. There are millstones on which the natives grind their corn and other foods. These are similar to the millstones in New Spain, except that they are stationary; and the women, if they have daughters, make them do the grinding.

These Indians are very clean people. The men bear burdens, but not the women. The manner of carrying loads, sleeping, eating, and sitting is the same as that of the Mexicans, for both men and women, except that they carry water in a different way. For this the Indians make and place on their heads a cushion of palm leaves, similar to those used in Old Castile, on top of which they place and carry the water jar. It is all very interesting.

The women part their hair in Spanish style. Some have light hair, which is surprising. The girls do not leave their rooms except when permitted by their parents. They are very obedient. They marry early; judging by what we saw, the women are given husbands when seventeen years of age. A man has one wife and no more. The women are the ones who spin, sew, weave and paint. Some of the women, like the men, bathe frequently. Their baths are as good as those of New Spain.

In all their valleys and other lands I have seen, there are one hundred pueblos. We named the region the province of San Felipe and took possession of it in the name of his Majesty by commission of his Excellency, Don Lorenzo Suárez de Mendoza, Count of Coruña, viceroy, governor and captain-general of New Spain.

Critical Thinking Questions

1. What can be learned from the document about relations between the Spanish and the Pueblo Indians around 1580?

2. What does the document tell us about Pueblo family structure?

Leo Africanus's Descriptions of African Societies

Leo Africanus was born El Hasan ben Muhammed el-Wazzan-ez-Zayyati in southern Spain in 1485. He was expelled, along with the rest of the country's Moors, in 1492 and settled in Morocco, where he pursued his education. He was later enslaved, brought to Italy, and presented to Pope Leo X. Leo sent him free, gave him his Latin name, and commissioned him to write a description of Africa.

The Kingdom of Mali

In this kingdom there is a large and ample village containing more than six thousand families, and named Mali, which is also the name of the whole kingdom. Here the king has his residence. The region itself yields great abundance of wheat, meat and cotton. Here are many craftsmen and merchants in all places: and yet the king honorably entertains all strangers. The inhabitants are rich and have plenty of merchandise. Here is a great number of temples, clergymen, and teachers, who read their lectures in the mosques because they have no colleges at all. The people of the region excel all other Negroes in wit, civility, and industry, and were the first that embraced the law of Muhammad....

The City of Timbuktu

All its houses are . . . cottages, built of mud and covered with thatch. However, there is a most stately mosque to be seen, whose walls are made of stone and lime, and a princely palace also constructed by the highly skilled craftsmen of Granada. Here there are many shops of artisans and merchants, especially of those who weave linen and cotton, and here Barbary merchants bring European cloth. The inhabitants, and especially resident aliens, are exceedingly rich, since the present king married both of his daughters to rich merchants. Here are many wells, containing sweet water. Whenever the Niger River overflows, they carry the water into town by means of sluices. This region yields great quantities of grain, cattle, milk, and butter, but salt is very scarce here, for it is brought here by land from Tegaza, which is five hundred miles away. When I was there, I saw one camel-load of salt sold for eighty ducats.

The rich king of Timbuktu has many plates and scepters of gold, some of which weigh 1,300 pounds, and he keeps a magnificent and well-furnished court. When he travels anywhere, he rides upon a camel, which is led by some of his noblemen. He does so likewise when going to war, and all his soldiers ride upon horses. Whoever wishes to speak to this king must first of all fall down before his feet and then taking up earth must sprinkle it on his own head and shoulders.... [The king] always has under arms 3,000 horsemen and a great number of foot soldiers who shoot poisoned arrows. They often skirmish with those who refuse to pay tribute and whomever they capture they sell to the merchants of Timbuktu. Here very few horses are bred.... Their best horses are brought out of North Africa. As soon as the king learns that any merchants have come to the town with horses, he commands that a certain number be

From *Leo Africanus, the History and Description of Africa*, London, Hakluyt Society, 1896.

brought before him. Choosing the best horse for himself, he pays a most liberal price for it. . . .

Here are great numbers of religious teachers, judges, scholars and other learned persons, who are bountifully maintained at the king's expense. Here too are brought various manuscripts or written books from Barbary, which are sold for more money than any other merchandise.

The coin of Timbuktu is gold, without any stamp or inscription, but in matters of small value they use certain shells from the kingdom of Persia. Four hundred of these are worth a ducat, and six pieces of Timbuktu's golden coin weigh two-thirds of an ounce.

The inhabitants are gentle and cheerful and spend a great part of the night in singing and dancing throughout the city streets. They keep large numbers of male and female slaves, and their town is greatly vulnerable to fire. At the time of my second visit, almost half the town burned down in the space of five hours.

The Town and Kingdom of Gao

Here are very rich merchants and to here journey continually large numbers of Negroes who purchase here cloth from Barbary and Europe. The town abounds in grain and meat but lacks wine, trees and fruits. However, there are plenty of melons, lemons and rice. Here there are many wells, which also contain very sweet and wholesome water. Here also is a certain place where slaves are sold, especially upon those days when merchants assemble. A young slave of fifteen years of age is sold for six ducats, and children are also sold.

The king of this region has a certain private palace in which he keeps a large number of concubines and slaves, who are watched by eunuchs. To guard his person he maintains a sufficient troop of horsemen and foot soldiers. Between the first gate of the palace and the inner part, there is a walled enclosure wherein the king personally decides all of his subjects' controversies. Although the king is most diligent in this regard and conducts all business in these matters, he has in his company counsellors and such other officers as his secretaries, treasurers, stewards and auditors.

It is a wonder to see the quality of merchandise that is daily brought here and how costly and sumptuous everything is. Horses purchased in Europe for ten ducats are sold here for forty and sometimes fifty ducats apiece. There is not European cloth so coarse as to sell for less than four ducats an ell. If it is anywhere near fine quality, they will give fifteen ducats for an ell, and an ell of the scarlet of Venice or of Turkish cloth is here worth thirty ducats. A sword is here valued at three or four crowns, and likewise are spears, bridles and similar commodities, and spices are all sold at a high rate. However, of all other items, salt is the most expensive.

The rest of this kingdom contains nothing but villages and hamlets inhabited by herdsmen and shepherds, who in winter cover their bodies with the skins of animals, but in summer they go naked, save for their private parts. . . . They are an ignorant and rude people, and you will scarcely find one learned person in the square of a hundred miles. They are continually burdened by heavy taxes; to the point that they scarcely have anything left on which to live.

The Kingdom of Borno

They have a most powerful prince. . . . He has in readiness as many as three thousand horsemen and a huge number of foot soldiers; for all his subjects are so serviceable and obedient to him, that whenever he commands them, they will arm themselves and will follow him wherever he leads them. They pay him no tribute except tithes on their grain; neither does the king have any revenues to support his state except the spoils he gets from his enemies by frequent invasions and assaults. He is in a state of perpetual hostility with a certain people who live beyond the desert of Seu, who in times past marching with a huge army of footsoldiers over the said desert, devastated a great part of the Kingdom of Borno. Whereupon the king sent for the merchants of Barbary and ordered them to bring him a great store of horses: for in this country they exchange horses for slaves, and sometimes give fifteen or twenty slaves for a horse. And by this means there were a great many horses bought although the merchants were forced to stay for their slaves until the king returned home as a conqueror with a great number of captives, and satisfied his creditors for his horses. Frequently it happens that the merchants must stay three months before the king returned from the wars. . . . Sometimes he does not bring home enough slaves to satisfy the merchants and sometimes they are forced to wait a whole year. . . . And yet the king seems marvelously rich, because his spurs, bridles, platters, dishes, pots and other vessels are made of gold. The king is extremely covetous and would rather pay his debts in slaves rather than gold.

Critical Thinking Questions

1. Does the author describe these societies in a positive or a negative light? Do you detect any bias on the part of the author?

2. What does this source tell us—directly or indirectly—about Timbuktu's political and social system?

3. What does the source tell us about trade and the economic life of these African societies?

4. Read the short section describing Mali. What can you infer about the likely natural resources, terrain, climate, or other geographical features of this area? (For example, is the area likely to be coastal or inland? Desert? Forest? Cleared?) Explain your answers.

The Chinese Emperor Addresses King George III of England
(1793)

In 1793 the Chinese emperor Qian'long (r. 1736–1795) was visited by Lord George Macartney, who headed a British delegation sent under the authority of England's King George III. Macartney came to request a major expansion of England's trade privileges with China. The emperor's reply is excerpted below.

An Imperial Edict to the King of England:

You, O King, are so inclined toward our civilization that you have sent a special envoy across the seas to bring to our Court your memorial of congratulations on the occasion of my birthday and to present your native products as an expression of your thoughtfulness. On perusing your memorial, so simply worded and sincerely conceived, I am impressed by your genuine respectfulness and friendliness and greatly pleased.

As to the request made in your memorial, O King, to send one of your nationals to stay at the Celestial Court to take care of your country's trade with China, this is not in harmony with the state system of our dynasty and will definitely not be permitted. Traditionally people of the European nations who wished to render some service under the Celestial Court have been permitted to come to the capital. But after their arrival they are obliged to wear Chinese court costumes, are placed in a certain residence, and are never allowed to return to their own countries. This is the established rule of the Celestial Dynasty with which presumably you, O King, are familiar. Now you, O King, wish to send one of your nationals to live in the capital, but he is not like the Europeans, who come to Peking as Chinese employees, live there and never return home again, nor can he be allowed to go and come and maintain any correspondence. This is indeed a useless undertaking.

Moreover the territory under the control of the Celestial Court is very large and wide. There are well-established regulations governing tributary envoys from the outer states to Peking, giving them provisions (of food and traveling expenses) by our post-houses and limiting their going and coming. There has never been a precedent for letting them do whatever they like. Now if you, O King, wish to have a representative in Peking, his language will be unintelligible and his dress different from the regulations; there is no place to accommodate him...

... The Celestial Court has pacified and possessed the territory within the four seas. Its sole aim is to do its utmost to achieve good government and to manage political affairs, attaching no value to strange jewels and precious objects. The various articles presented by you, O King, this time are accepted by my special order to the office in charge of such functions in consideration of the offerings having come from a long distance with sincere good wishes. As a matter of fact, the virtue and prestige of

From *China's Response to the West: A Documentary Survey*, Harvard University Press.

the Celestial Dynasty having spread far and wide, the kings of the myriad nations come by land and sea with all sorts of precious things. Consequently there is nothing we lack, as your principal envoy and others have themselves observed. We have never set much store on strange or ingenious objects, nor do we need any more of your country's manufactures. . . .

Critical Thinking Questions

1. How would you characterize the attitude of the Chinese Emperor and court (who wrote the letter) toward the English? Toward foreigners in general?

2. Put yourself into the shoes of England's King George III and comment on any passages that offend you, even if only slightly. Say why.

3. What is the Chinese Emperor's response to the English request for an expansion of trade privileges with China? What justification does the emperor provide?

Absolutism & Constitutionalism

James I of England Speaks to Parliament (1610)

Duc de Saint-Simon, The Court of Louis XIV

Peter the Great: Westernizing Decrees (1701)

The English Bill of Rights (1689)

John Locke, The Second Treatise of Government *(1690)*

James I of England Speaks to Parliament
(1610)

James VI of Scotland ruled also as James I of England (1603–1625). His views on the nature and purpose of royal power are made clear in the following extract.

A Speech to Parliament (1610)

... The state of monarchy is the supremest thing upon earth, for kings are not only God's lieutenants upon earth and sit upon God's throne, but even by God himself they are called gods. There be three principal [comparisons] that illustrate the state of monarchy: one taken out of the word of God, and the two other out of the grounds of policy and philosophy. In the Scriptures kings are called gods, and so their power after a certain relation compared to the Divine power. Kings are also compared to fathers of families; for a king is truly *parens patriae* [parent of the country], the politic father of his people. And lastly, kings are compared to the head of this microcosm of the body of man ...

I conclude then this point touching the power of kings with this axiom of divinity, that as to dispute what God may do is blasphemy ... so is it sedition in subjects to dispute what a king may do in the height of his power. But just kings will ever be willing to declare what they will do, if they will not incur the curse of God. I will not be content that my power be disputed upon, but I shall ever be willing to make the reason appear of all my doings, and rule my actions according to my laws ...

Now the second general ground whereof I am to speak concerns the matter of grievances ... First then, I am not to find fault that you inform yourselves of the particular just grievances of the people; nay I must tell you, ye can neither be just nor faithful to me or to your countries that trust and employ you, if you do it not ... But I would wish you to be careful to avoid [these] things in the matter of grievances.

First, that you do not meddle with the main points of government; that is my craft ... to meddle with that, were to lessen me. I am now an old king ... I must not be taught my office. Secondly, I would not have you meddle with such ancient rights of mine as I have received from my predecessors, possessing them *more* (as ancestral customs): such things I would be sorry should be accounted for grievances. All novelties are dangerous as well in a politic as in a natural body, and therefore I would be loath to be quarreled in my ancient rights and possessions: for that were to judge me unworthy of that which my predecessors had and left me.

From *Selected Statutes and Other Constitutional Documents Illustrative of the Reigns of Elizabeth and James I*, Oxford: Clarendon Press, 1906.

Critical Thinking Questions

1. What limitations on his power does James recognize, either explicitly or implicitly?

2. According to James I, what is the relationship between God and kings?

3. What can you infer from the document about why James might have felt it necessary to make such a speech before Parliament?

Duc de Saint-Simon, The Court of Louis XIV

Louis de Rouvroy, duc de Saint-Simon (1675–1755), was a French diplomat and writer who lived at the magnificent Palace of Versailles during the reign of Louis XIV. Known as the Sun King, Louis XIV was the epitome of an absolute ruler and successfully created one of the most centralized states in Europe. In his famous Memoirs, *from which the following excerpt is taken, the Duc de Saint-Simon provides valuable information about daily life at court as well as great insights into the methods Louis XIV used to control the French nobility and other opponents of his centralizing efforts.*

Life at Versailles

Very early in the reign of Louis XIV the Court was removed from Paris, never to return. The troubles of the minority had given him a dislike to that city; his enforced and surreptitious flight from it still rankled in his memory; he did not consider himself safe there, and thought cabals would be more easily detected if the Court was in the country, where the movements and temporary absences of any of its members would be more easily noticed.... No doubt that he was also influenced by the feeling that he would be regarded with greater awe and veneration when no longer exposed every day to the gaze of the multitude.

His love-affair with Mademoiselle de la Vallière, which at first was covered as far as possible with a veil of mystery, was the cause of frequent excursions to Versailles. This was at that time a small country house, built by Louis XIII to avoid the unpleasant necessity, which had sometimes befallen him, of sleeping at a wretched wayside tavern or in a windmill, when benighted out hunting in the forest of St. Leger.... The visits of Louis XIV becoming more frequent, he enlarged the *château* by degrees till its immense buildings afforded better accommodation for the Court than was to be found at St. Germain, where most of the courtiers had to put up with uncomfortable lodgings in the town. The Court was therefore removed to Versailles in 1682, not long before the Queen's death. The new building contained an infinite number of rooms for courtiers, and the King liked the grant of these rooms to be regarded as a coveted privilege.

He availed himself of the frequent festivities at Versailles, and his excursions to other places, as a means of making the courtiers assiduous in their attendance and anxious to please him; for he nominated beforehand those who were to take part in them, and could thus gratify some and inflict a snub on others. He was conscious that the substantial favours he has to bestow were not nearly sufficient to produce a continual effect; he had therefore to invent imaginary ones, and no one was so clever in devising petty distinctions and preferences which aroused jealously and emulation. The visits to Marly later on were very useful to him in this way; also those to Trianon, where certain ladies, chosen beforehand, were admitted to his table. It was another distinction to

---

From *The Memoirs of the Duke de Saint-Simon*, ed. F. Arkwright (New York Brentano's, n.d.), Vol. V, pp. 254, 259-63, 271-274, 276-278.

hold his candlestick at his *coucher*; as soon as he had finished his prayers he used to name the courtier to whom it was to be handed, always choosing one of the highest rank among those present....

Not only did he expect all persons of distinction to be in continual attendance at Court, but he was quick to notice the absence of those of inferior degree; at his *lever*, his *coucher*, his meals, in the gardens of Versailles (the only place where the courtiers in general were allowed to follow him), he used to cast his eyes to right and left; nothing escaped him, he saw everybody. If any one habitually living at Court absented himself he insisted on knowing the reason; those who came there only for flying visits had also to give a satisfactory explanation; any one who seldom or never appeared there was certain to incur his displeasure. If asked to bestow a favour on such persons he would reply haughtily: "I do not know him"; of such as rarely presented themselves he would say, "He is a man I never see"; and from these judgements there was no appeal.

He always took great pains to find out what was going on in public places, in society, in private houses, even family secrets, and maintained an immense number of spies and tale-bearers. These were of all sorts; some did not know that their reports were carried to him; others did know it; there were others, again, who used to write to him directly, through channels which he prescribed; others who were admitted by the backstairs and saw him in his private room. Many a man in all ranks of life was ruined by these methods, often very unjustly, without ever being able to discover the reason; and when the King had once taken a prejudice against a man, he hardly ever got over it....

No one understood better than Louis XIV the art of enhancing the value of a favour by his manner of bestowing it; he knew how to make the most of a word, a smile, even of a glance. If he addressed any one, were it but to ask a trifling question or make some commonplace remark, all eyes were turned on the person so honored; it was a mark of favour which always gave rise to comment....

He loved splendour, magnificence, and profusion in all things, and encouraged similar tastes in his Court; to spend money freely on equipages and buildings, on feasting and at cards, was a sure way to gain his favour, perhaps to obtain the honour of a word from him. Motives of policy had something to do with this; by making expensive habits the fashion, and, for people in a certain position, a necessity, he compelled his courtiers to live beyond their income, and gradually reduced them to depend on his bounty for the means of subsistence. This was a plague which, once introduced, became a scourge to the whole country, for it did not take long to spread to Paris, and hence to the armies and the provinces; so that a man of any position is now estimated entirely according to his expenditure on his table and other luxuries. This folly, sustained by pride and ostentation, has already produced widespread confusion; it threatens to end in nothing short of ruin and a general overthrow.

Critical Thinking Questions

1. According to the source, why did Louis XIV move the French court from Paris to Versailles?

2. What class in society can we infer took part in life at court? What privileges were available to them at Versailles?

3. Based on the author's description of court life, what methods or techniques did Louis XIV use to control courtiers at Versailles?

4. What is the attitude of the Duc de Saint-Simon toward Louis XIV?

Peter the Great: Westernizing Decrees
(1701)

Russian tsar Peter the Great ruled from 1682 to 1725. He was the first Russian ruler to correctly perceive the importance of Western advances and to attempt to effect relevant Westernizing changes within his domains. Among Peter's greatest achievements were the creation of the Russian navy and the establishment of a new capital, his "window on the West," St. Petersburg. A section of Peter's Westernizing decrees follows.

Decree on Western Dress (1701)

Western dress shall be worn by all the boyars, members of our councils and of our court... gentry of Moscow, secretaries... provincial gentry, gosti, government officials, strel'tsy, members of the guilds purveying for our household, citizens of Moscow of all ranks, and residents of provincial cities... excepting the clergy and peasant tillers of the soil. The upper dress shall be of French or Saxon cut, and the lower dress...—(including) waistcoat, trousers, boots, shoes, and hats—shall be of the German type. They shall also ride German saddles. Likewise the womenfolk of all ranks, including the priests', deacons', and church attendants' wives, the wives of the dragoons, the soldiers, and the strel'tsy, and their children, shall wear Western dresses, hats, jackets, and underwear—undervests and petticoats—and shoes. From now on no one of the above-mentioned is to wear Russian dress or Circassian coats, sheepskin coats, or Russian peasant coats, trousers, boots, and shoes. It is also forbidden to ride Russian saddles, and the craftsmen shall not manufacture them or sell them at the marketplaces.

Decree on Shaving (1705)

A decree to be published in Moscow and in all the provincial cities; Henceforth, in accordance with this, His Majesty's decree, all court attendants... provincial service men, government officials of all ranks, military men, all the gosti, members of the wholesale merchants' guild, and members of the guilds purveying for our household must shave their beards and moustaches. But, if it happens that some of them do not wish to shave their beards and moustaches, let a yearly tax be collected from such persons; from court attendants... provincial service men, military men, and government officials of all ranks—60 rubles per person; from the gosti and members of the wholesale merchants' guild of the first class—100 rubles per person; from members of the wholesale merchants' guild of the middle and the lower class (and)... from (other) merchants and townsfolk—60 rubles per person; ... from townsfolk (of the lower rank), boyars' servants, stagecoachmen, waggoners, church attendants (with the exception of priests and deacons), and from Moscow residents of all ranks—30 rubles per

---

From *A Sourcebook for Russian History: From Early Times to 1917*, by A. Vernadsky. Reprinted by permission of Yale University Press.

person. Special badges shall be issued to them from the Administrator of Land Affairs of Public Order ... which they must wear.... As for the peasants, let a toll of two half-copecks per beard be collected at the town gates each time they enter or leave a town; and do not let the peasants pass the town gates, into or out of town, without paying this toll.

Decree on Compulsory Education of the Russian Nobility (1714)

Send to every administrative district some persons from mathematical schools to teach the children of the nobility—except those of freeholders and government clerks—mathematics and geometry; as a penalty for evasion establish a rule that no one will be allowed to marry unless he learns these subjects. Inform all prelates to issue no marriage certificates to those who are ordered to go to schools....

The Great Sovereign has decreed; in all administrative districts children between the ages of ten and fifteen of the nobility, of government clerks, and of lesser officials, except those of freeholders, must be taught mathematics and some geometry. Toward that end, students should be sent from mathematical schools as teachers, several into each administrative district to prelates and to renowned monasteries to establish schools. During their instruction these teachers should be given food and financial remuneration ... from district revenues set aside for that purpose by personal orders of His Imperial Majesty. No fees should be collected from students. When they have mastered the material, they should then be given certificates written in their own handwriting. When the students are released they ought to pay one ruble each for their training. Without these certificates they should not be allowed to marry nor receive marriage certificates.

An Instruction to Russian Students Abroad Studying Navigation (1714)

1. Learn how to draw plans and charts and how to use the compass and other naval indicators.
2. Learn how to navigate a vessel in battle as well as in a simple maneuver, and learn how to use all appropriate tools and instruments; namely, sails, ropes, and oars, and the like matters, on row boats and other vessels.
3. Discover as much as possible how to put ships to sea during a naval battle. Those who cannot succeed in this effort must diligently ascertain what action should be taken by the vessels that do and those that do not put to sea during such a situation (naval battle). Obtain from foreign naval officers written statements, bearing their signatures and seals, of how adequately you are prepared for naval duties.
4. If, upon his return, anyone wishes to receive from the Tsar greater favors for himself, he should learn, in addition to the above enumerated instructions, how to construct those vessels abroad in which he would like to demonstrate his skills.
5. Upon his return to Moscow, every foreign-trained Russian should bring with him at his own expense, for which he will later be reimbursed, at least two experienced masters of naval science. They the returnees will be assigned soldiers, one soldier per returnee, to teach them what they have learned abroad. And if they do not wish to accept soldiers, they may teach their acquaintances or their own people. The treasury will pay for transportation and maintenance of soldiers. And if anyone other than soldiers learns the art of navigation the treasury will pay 100 rubles for the maintenance of every such individual.

Critical Thinking Questions

1. Looking at the first decree, why do you think Peter thought it important to tell people how to dress? And why might he have chosen "French or Saxon" styles in particular?

2. Which of the four decrees given here do you think might have been the most controversial among his subjects? Why?

3. Which decree do you think would have been the most useful? Why?

The English Bill of Rights
(1689)

The Bill of Rights is a landmark of constitutional history and the third major character of English freedoms after the Magna Carta (1215) and Petition of Right (1628). Signed by King William III and Queen Mary following the Glorious Revolution in 1689, it limited the powers of the monarchy and protected Parliament's prerogatives.

An Act declareing the Rights and Liberties of the Subject and Setleing the Succession of the Crowne.

I. Whereas the Lords Spirituall and Temporall and Commons assembled at Westminster lawfully fully and freely representing all the Estates of the People of this Realme did upon the thirteenth day of February in the yeare of our Lord one thousand six hundred eighty eight present unto their Majesties then called and known by the Names and Stile of William and Mary Prince and Princesse of Orange being present in their proper Persons a certaine Declaration in Writing made by the said Lords and Commons in the Words following viz.

Whereas the late King James the Second by the Assistance of diverse evill Councellors Judges and Ministers imployed by him did endeavour to subvert and extirpate the Protestant Religion and the Lawes and Liberties of this Kingdome.

By Assumeing and Excerciseing a Power of Dispensing with and Suspending of Lawes and the Execution of Lawes without Consent of Parlyament.

By Committing and Prosecuting diverse Worthy Prelates for humbly Petitioning to bee excused from Concurring to the said Assumed Power.

By issueing and causeing to be executed a Commission under the Great Seale for Erecting a Court called The Court of Commissioners for Ecclesiasticall Causes.

By Levying Money for and to the Use of the Crowne by pretence of Prerogative for other time and in other manner then the same was granted by Parlyament.

By raising and keeping a Standing Army within this Kingdome in time of Peace without Consent of Parlyament and Quartering Soldiers contrary to Law.

By causing severall good Subjects being Protestants to be disarmed at the same time when Papists were both Armed and Imployed contrary to Law.

By Violating the Freedome of Election of Members to Serve in Parlyament.

By Prosecutions in the Court of Kings Bench for Matters and Causes cognizable onely in Parlyament and by diverse other Arbitrary and Illegal Courses.

And whereas of late yeares Partiall Corrupt and Unqualifyed Persons have beene returned and served on Juryes in Tryalls and Particularly diverse Jurors in Tryalls for High Treason which were not Freeholders,

And excessive Baile hath beene required of Persons committed in Criminall Cases to elude the Benefitt of the Lawes made for the Liberty of the Subjects.

And excessive Fines have beene imposed.

And illegall and cruell Punishments inflicted.

From *The Law and Working of the Constitution: Documents 1660–1914*, London, Adam & Charles Black.

And severall Grants and Promises made of Fines or Forfeitures before any Conviction or Judgement against the Persons upon whome the same were to be levyed.

All which are utterly and directly contrary to the knowne Lawes and Statutes and Freedome of this Realme.

And whereas the said late King James the Second haveing Abdicated the Government and the Throne being thereby Vacant His Highnesse the Prince of Orange (whome it hath pleased Almighty God to make the glorious Instrument of Delivering this Kingdome from Popery and Arbitrary Power) did (by the Advice of the Lords Spirituall and Temporall and diverse principall Persons of the Commons) cause Letters to be written to the Lords Spirituall and Temporall being Protestants and other Letters to the severall Countyes Cityes Universities Burroughs and Cinque Ports for the Choosing of such Persons to represent them as were of right to be sent to Parlyament to meete and sitt at Westminster upon the two and twentyeth day of January in this Yeare One thousand six hundred eighty and eight in order to such an Establishment as that their Religion Lawes and Liberties might not againe be in danger of being Subverted, Upon which Letters Elections haveing beene accordingly made.

And thereupon the said Lords Spirituall and Temporall and Commons pursuant to their respective Letters and Elections being now assembled in a full and free Representative of this Nation taking into their most serious Consideration the best meanes for attaining the Ends aforesaid Doe in the first place (as their Auncestors in like Case have usually done) for the Vindicating and Asserting their auntient Rights and Liberties, Declare

That the pretended Power of Suspending of Laws or the Execution of Laws by Regall Authority without Consent of Parlyament is illegall.

That the pretended Power of Dispensing with Laws or the Execution of Laws by Regall Authoritie as it hath beene assumed and exercised of late is illegall.

That the Commission for erecting the late Court of Commissioners for Ecclesiasticall Causes and all other Commissions and Courts of like nature are Illegall and Pernicious.

That levying Money for or to the Use of the Crowne by pretence of Prerogative without Grant of Parlyament for longer time or in other manner then the same is or shall be granted is Illegall.

That it is the Right of the Subjects to petition the King and all Commitments and Prosecutions for such Petitioning are Illegall.

That the raising or keeping a standing Army within the Kingdome in time of Peace unlesse it be with Consent of Parlyament is against Law.

That the Subjects which are Protestants may have Arms for their Defence suitable to their Conditions and as allowed by Law.

That Election of Members of Parlyament ought to be free.

That the Freedome of Speech and Debates or Proceedings in Parlyament ought not to be impeached or questioned in any Court or Place out of Parlyament.

That excessive Baile ought not to be required nor excessive Fines imposed nor cruell and unusuall Punishments inflicted.

That Jurors ought to be duely impannelled and returned and Jurors which passe upon Men in Trialls for High Treason ought to be Freeholders.

That all Grants and Promises of Fines and Forfeitures of particular persons before Conviction are illegall and void.

And that for Redresse of all Grievances and for the amending strengthening and preserving of the Lawes Parlyaments ought to be held frequently.

And they doe Claime Demand and Insist upon all and singular the Premises as their undoubted Rights and Liberties and that noe Declarations Judgements Doeings or Proceedings to the Prejudice of the People in any of the said Premisses ought in any wise to be drawne hereafter into Consequence or Example. To which Demand of their Rights they are particularly encouraged by the Declaration of his Highnesse the Prince of Orange as being the onely meanes for obtaining a full Redresse and Remedy therein. Haveing therefore an intire Confidence That his said Highnesse the Prince of Orange will perfect the Deliverance soe farr advanced by him and will still preserve them from the Violation of their Rights which they have here asserted and from all other Attempts upon their Religion Rights and Liberties. The said Lords Spirituall and Temporall and Commons assembled at Westminster doe Resolve That William and Mary Prince and Princesse of Orange be and be declared King and Queene of England France and Ireland and the Dominions thereunto belonging to hold the Crowne and Royall Dignity of the said Kingdomes and Dominions to them the said Prince and Princesse dureing their

Lives and the Life of the Survivour of them And that the sole and full Exercise of the Regall Power be onely in and executed by the said Prince of Orange in the Names of the said Prince and Princesse dureing their joynt Lives And after their Deceases the said Crowne and Royall Dignitie of the said Kingdoms and Dominions to be to the Heires of the Body of the said Princesse And for default of such Issue to the Princesse Anne of Denmarke and the Heires of her Body And for default of such Issue to the Heires of the Body of the said Prince of Orange. And the Lords Spirituall and Temporall and Commons doe pray the said Prince and Princesse to accept the same accordingly.

And that the Oathes hereafter mentioned be taken by all Persons of whome the Oathes of Allegiance and Supremacy might be required by Law instead of them And that the said Oathes of Allegiance and Supremacy be abrogated.

I A B doe sincerely promise and sweare That I will be faithfull and beare true Allegiance to their Majestyes King William and Queene Mary Soe helpe me God.

I A B doe sweare That I doe from my Heart Abhorr, Detest and Abjure as Impious and Hereticall this damnable Doctrine and Position That Princes Excommunicated or Deprived by the Pope or any Authority of the See of Rome may be deposed or murdered by their Subjects or any other whatsoever. And I doe declare That noe Forreigne Prince Person Prelate, State or Potentate hath or ought to have any Jurisdiction Power Superiority Preeminence or Authoritie Ecclesiasticall or Spirituall within this Realme So helpe me God.

Upon which their said Majestyes did accept the Crowne and Royall Dignitie of the Kingdoms of England France and Ireland and the Dominions thereunto belonging according to the Resolution and Desire of the said Lords and Commons contained in the said Declaration. And thereupon their Majestyes were pleased That the said Lords Spirituall and Temporall and Commons being the two Houses of Parlyament should continue to sitt and with their Majestyes Royall Concurrence make effectual Provision for the Setlement of the Religion Lawes and Liberties of this Kingdome soe that the same for the future might not be in danger againe of being subverted, To which the said Lords Spirituall and Temporall and Commons did agree and proceede to act accordingly. Now in pursuance of the Premisses the said Lords Spirituall and Temporall and Commons in Parlyament assembled for the ratifying confirming and establishing the said Declaration and the Articles Clauses Matters and Things therein contained by the Force of a Law made in due Forme by Authority of Parlyament doe pray that it may be declared and enacted That all and singular the Rights and Liberties asserted and claimed in the said Declaration are the true auntient and indubitable Rights and Liberties of the People of this Kingdome and soe shall be esteemed allowed adjudged deemed and taken to be and that all and every the particulars aforesaid shall be firmly and strictly holden and observed as they are expressed in the said Declaration And all Officers and Ministers whatsoever shall serve their Majestyes and their Successors according to the same in all times to come. And the said Lords Spirituall and Temporall and Commons seriously considering how it hath pleased Almighty God in his marvellous Providence and mercifull Goodness to this Nation to provide and preserve their said Majestyes Royall Persons most happily to Raigne over us upon the Throne of their Auncestors for which they render unto him from the bottome of their Hearts their humblest Thanks and Praises doe truely firmly and assuredly and in the Sincerity of their Hearts thinke and doe hereby recognize acknowledge and declare That King James the Second haveing abdicated the Government and their Majestyes haveing accepted the Crowne and Royall Dignity as aforesaid Their said Majestyes did become were are and of right ought to be by the Lawes of this Realme our Soveraigne Liege Lord and Lady King and Queene of England France and Ireland and the Dominions thereunto belonging in and to whose Princely Persons the Royall State Crowne and Dignity of the said Realmes with all Honours Stiles Titles Regalities Prerogatives Powers Jurisdictions and Authorities to the same belonging and appertaining are most fully rightfully and intirely invested and incorporated united and annexed And for preventing all Questions and Divisions in this Realme by reason of any pretended Titles to the Crowne and for preserveing a Certainty in the Succession thereof in and upon which the Unity Peace Tranquillity and Safety of this Nation doth under God wholly consist and depend The said Lords Spirituall and Temporall and Commons doe beseech their Majestyes That it may be enacted established and declared That the Crowne and Regall Government of the said Kingdoms and Dominions with all and singular the Premisses thereunto belonging and appertaining shall bee and continue to their said

Majestyes and the Survivour of them dureing their Lives and the Life of the Survivour of them And that the entire perfect and full Exercise of the Regall Power and Government be onely in and executed by his Majestie in the Names of both their Majestyes dureing their joynt Lives And after their deceases the said Crowne and Premisses shall be and remaine to the Heires of the Body of her Majestie and for default of such Issue to her Royall Highnesse the Princess Anne of Denmarke and the Heires of her Body and for default of such Issue to the Heires of the Body of his said Majestie And thereunto the said Lords Spirituall and Temporall and Commons doe in the Name of all the People aforesaid most humbly and faithfully submitt themselves their Heires and Posterities for ever and doe faithfully promise That they will stand to maintaine and defend their said Majesties and alsoe the Limitation and Succession of the Crowne herein specified and contained to the utmost of their Powers with their Lives and Estates against all Persons whatsoever that shall attempt any thing to the contrary. And whereas it hath beene found by Experience that it is inconsistent with the Safety and Welfaire of this Protestant Kingdome to be governed by a Popish Prince or by any King or Queene marrying a Papist the said Lords Spirituall and Temporall and Commons doe further pray that it may be enacted That all and every person and persons that is are or shall be reconciled to or shall hold Communion with the See or Church of Rome or shall professe the Popish Religion or shall marry a Papist shall be excluded and be for ever uncapeable to inherit possesse or enjoy the Crowne and Government of this Realme and Ireland and the Dominions thereunto belonging or any part of the same or to have use or excercise any Regall Power Authoritie or Jurisdiction within the same [And in all and every such Case or Cases the People of these Realmes shall be and are hereby absolved of their Allegiance] And the said Crowne and Government shall from time to time descend to and be enjoyed by such person or persons being Protestants as should have inherited and enjoyed the same in case the said person or persons soe reconciled holding Communion or Professing or Marrying as aforesaid were naturally dead [And that every King and Queene of this Realme who at any time hereafter shall come to and succeede in the Imperiall Crowne of this Kingdome shall on the first day of the meeting of the first Parlyament next after his or her comeing to the Crowne sitting in his or her Throne in the House of Peeres in the presence of the Lords and Commons therein assembled or at his or her Coronation before such person or persons who shall administer the Coronation Oath to him or her at the time of his or her takeing the said Oath (which shall first happen) make subscribe and audibly repeate the Declaration mentioned in the Statute made in the thirtyeth yeare of the Raigne of King Charles the Second Entituled An Act for the more effectuall Preserveing the Kings Person and Government by disableing Papists from sitting in either House of Parlyament. But if it shall happen that such King or Queene upon his or her Succession to the Crowne of this Realme shall be under the Age of twelve yeares then every such King or Queene shall make subscribe and audibly repeate the said Declaration at his or her Coronation or the first day of the meeting of the first Parlyament as aforesaid which shall first happen after such King or Queene shall have attained the said Age of twelve years.] All which their Majestyes are contented and pleased shall be declared enacted and established by authoritie of this present Parliament and shall stand remaine and be the Law of this Realme for ever And the same are by their said Majestyes by and with the advice and consent of the Lords Spirituall and Temporall and Commons in Parlyament assembled and by the authoritie of the same declared enacted and established accordingly.

II. And bee it further declared and enacted by the Authoritie aforesaid That from and after this present Session of Parlyament noe Dispensation by Non obstante of or to any Statute or any part thereof shall be allowed but that the same shall be held void and of noe effect Except a Dispensation be allowed of in such Statute and except in such Cases as shall be specially provided for by one or more Bill or Bills to be passed dureing this present Session of Parliament.

III. Provided that noe Charter or Grant or Pardon granted before the three and twentyeth Day of October in the yeare of our Lord one thousand six hundred eighty nine shall be any wayes impeached or invalidated by this Act but that the same shall be and remaine of the same force and effect in Law and noe other then as if this Act had never beene made.

Critical Thinking Questions

1. What general rights were accorded to all Englishmen by this bill? What freedoms were not granted to all?

2. What can you infer from the document about religious divisions and tensions in England at the time?

John Locke, The Second Treatise of Government
(1690)

John Locke (1634–1704) was a middle-class Englishman who wrote influential pieces on government and education. He supported the revolutions that changed England's absolute monarchy into a constitutional one during the seventeenth century. His Second Treatise of Government *(1690) is excerpted here.*

4. To understand political power right and derive it from its original, we must consider what state all men are naturally in, and that is a state of perfect freedom to order their actions and dispose of their possessions and persons as they think fit, within the bounds of the law of nature, without asking leave or depending upon the will of any other man.

6. But though this be a state of liberty, yet it is not a state of license; though man in that state has [sic] an uncontrollable liberty to dispose of his person or possessions, yet he has not liberty to destroy himself, or so much as any creature in his possession, but where some nobler use than its bare preservation calls for it. The state of nature has a law of nature to govern it, which obliges every one; and reason, which is that law, teaches all mankind who will but consult it that, being all equal and independent, no one ought to harm one another in his life, health, liberty, or possessions; for men being all the workmanship of one omnipotent and infinitely wise Maker—all the servants of one sovereign master, sent into the world by his order, and about his business—they are his property whose workmanship they are, made to last during his, not one another's, pleasure; and being furnished with like faculties, sharing all in one community of nature, there cannot be supposed any such subordination among us that may authorize us to destroy another, as if we were made for one another's uses as the inferior ranks of creatures are for ours. Every one, as he is bound to preserve himself and not to quit his station wilfully, so by the like reason, when his own preservation comes not in competition, ought he, as much as he can, to preserve the rest of mankind, and may not, unless it be to do justice to an offender, take away or impair the life, or what tends to the preservation of the life, the liberty, health, limb, or goods of another.

26. God, who has given the world to men in common, has also given them reason to make use of it to the best advantage of life and convenience. The earth and all that is therein is given to men for the support and comfort of their being. And though all the fruits it naturally produces and beasts it feeds belong to mankind in common, as they are produced by the spontaneous hand of nature; and nobody has originally a private dominion exclusive of the rest of mankind in any of them, as they are thus in their natural state; yet, being given for the use of men, there must of necessity be a means to appropriate them some way or other before they can be of any

---

From *Second Treatise of Government*, by John Locke, Pearson Education, Inc.

use or at all beneficial to any particular man. The fruit or venison which nourishes the wild Indian, who knows no enclosure and is still a tenant in common, must be his, and so his, i.e., a part of him, that another can no longer have any right to it before it can do him any good for the support of his life.

27. Though the earth and all inferior creatures be common to all men, yet every man has a property in his own person; this nobody has any right to but himself. The labor of his body and the work of his hands, we may say, are properly his. Whatsoever then he removes out of the state that nature has provided and left it in, he has mixed his labor with, and joined to it something that is his own, and thereby makes it his property. It being by him removed from the common state nature has placed it in, it has by this labor something annexed to it that excludes the common right of other men. For this labor being the unquestionable property of the laborer, no man but he can have a right to what that is once joined to, at least where there is enough and as good left in common for others.

95. Men being, as has been said, by nature all free, equal, and independent, no one can be put out of this estate and subjected to the political power of another without his own consent. The only way whereby any one divests himself of his natural liberty and puts on the bonds of civil society is by agreeing with other men to join and unite into a community for their comfortable, safe, and peaceable living one amongst another, in a secure enjoyment of their properties and a greater security against any that are not of it. This any number of men may do, because it injures not the freedom of the rest; they are left as they were in the liberty of the state of nature. When any number of men have so consented to make one community or government, they are thereby presently incorporated and make one body politic wherein the majority have a right to act and conclude the rest.

123. If man in the state of nature be so free, as has been said, if he be absolute lord of his own person and possessions, equal to the greatest, and subject to nobody, why will he part with his freedom, why will he give up his empire and subject himself to the dominion and control of any other power? To which it is obvious to answer that though in the state of nature he has such a right, yet the enjoyment of it is very uncertain and constantly exposed to the invasion of others; for all being kings as much as he, every man his equal, and the greater part no strict observers of equity and justice, the enjoyment of the property he has in this state is very unsafe, very unsecure. This makes him willing to quit a condition which, however free, is full of fears and continual dangers; and it is not without reason that he seeks out and is willing to join in society with others who are already united, or have a mind to unite, for the mutual preservation of their lives, liberties, and estates, which I call by the general name 'property.'

124. The great and chief end, therefore, of men's uniting into commonwealths and putting themselves under government is the preservation of their property. . . .

199. As usurpation is the exercise of power which another has a right to, so tyranny is the exercise of power beyond right, which nobody can have a right to. And this is making use of the power any one has in his hands, not for the good of those who are under it, but for his own private separate advantage—when the governor, however entitled, makes not the law, but his will, the rule, and his commands and actions are not directed to the preservation of the properties of his people, but the satisfaction of his own ambition, revenge, covetousness, or any other irregular passion.

202. Wherever law ends, tyranny begins if the law be transgressed to another's harm. And whosoever in authority exceeds the power given him by the law, and makes use of the force he has under his command to compass that upon the subject which the law allows not, ceases in that to be a magistrate and, acting without authority, may be opposed as any other man who by force invades the right of another. This is acknowledged in subordinate magistrates. He that has authority to seize my person in the street may be opposed as a thief and a robber if he endeavors to break into my house to execute a writ, notwithstanding that I know he has such a warrant and such a legal authority as will empower him to arrest me abroad. And why this should not hold in the highest as well as in the most inferior magistrate, I would gladly be informed. Is it reasonable that the eldest brother, because he has the greatest part of his father's estate, should thereby have a right to take away any of his younger brother's portions? Or that a rich man who possessed a whole country should from thence have a right to seize, when he pleased, the cottage and garden of his poor neighbor? The being rightfully possessed of great power and riches, exceedingly beyond the greatest part of the sons of Adam, is so far from being an excuse, much less a reason, for rapine and oppression, which the endamaging another without authority is, that it is a great aggravation of it; for the exceeding the bounds of authority is no more a right in a great than in a petty officer, no more justifiable in a king than a constable; but is so much the worse in him in that he has more trust put in him, has already a much greater share than the rest of his brethren, and is supposed, from the advantages of his education, employment, and counselors, to be more knowing in the measures of right and wrong.

222. The reason why men enter into society is the preservation of their property; and the end why they choose and authorize a legislative is that there may be laws made and rules set as guards and fences to the properties of all the members of the society to limit the power and moderate the dominion of every part and member of the society; for since it can never be supposed to be the will of the society that the legislative should have a power to destroy that which every one designs to secure by entering into society, and for which the people submitted themselves to legislators of their own making. Whenever the legislators endeavor to take away and destroy the property of the people, or to reduce them to slavery under arbitrary power, they put themselves into a state of war with the people who are thereupon absolved from any further obedience, and are left to the common refuge which God has provided for all men against force and violence. Whensoever, therefore, the legislative shall transgress this fundamental rule of society, and either by ambition, fear, folly, or corruption, endeavor to grasp themselves, or put into the hands of any other, an absolute power over the lives, liberties, and estates of the people, by this breach of trust they forfeit the power the people had put into their hands for quite contrary ends, and it devolves to the people, who have a right to resume their original liberty and, by the establishment of a new legislative, such as they shall think fit, provide for their own safety and security, which is the end for which they are in society.

Critical Thinking Questions

1. According to Locke, what is man's natural state?

2. What, specifically, does the "law of nature" teach us all?

3. How is common property turned into private property, according to Locke?

4. Why do men willingly "enter into society" and subject themselves to the control of the government? What happens when a government exceeds its power and becomes tyrannical?

The Scientific Revolution & Enlightenment

Copernicus Gives His Reasons for Delaying Publication of
On the Revolutions *(1543)*

Francis Bacon and the Method of Science (1620)

Voltaire, A Treatise on Toleration *(1763)*

Adam Smith's Free-Market Capitalism (1776)

Copernicus Gives His Reasons for Delaying Publication of On the Revolutions
(1543)

Nicolaus Copernicus (1473–1543) was a mathematician and an astronomer born in Poland. He was the first person in modern times to propose that the sun, not the earth, is at the center of the universe and that the earth spins on its axis. Copernicus kept his "heliocentric" theory to himself for many years. Only toward the very end of his life did he agree to publication. Here he gives his reasons.

To His Holiness, Pope Paul III, Nicolaus Copernicus' Preface to His Books on the Revolutions

I can readily imagine, Holy Father, that as soon as some people hear that in this volume, which I have written about the revolutions of the spheres of the universe, I ascribe certain motions to the terrestrial globe, they will shout that I must be immediately repudiated together with this belief. For I am not so enamored of my own opinions that I disregard what others may think of them. I am aware that a philosopher's ideas are not subject to the judgment of ordinary persons, because it is his endeavor to seek the truth in all things, to the extent permitted to human reason by God. Yet I hold that completely erroneous views should be shunned. Those who know that the consensus of many centuries has sanctioned the conception that the earth remains at rest in the middle of the heaven as its center would, I reflected, regard it as an insane pronouncement if I made the opposite assertion that the earth moves. Therefore I debated with myself for a long time whether to publish the volume which I wrote to prove the earth's motion or rather to follow the example of the Pythagoreans and certain others, who used to transmit philosophy's secrets only to kinsmen and friends, not in writing but by word of mouth. . . . And they did so, it seems to me, not, as some suppose, because they were in some way jealous about their teachings, which would be spread around; on the contrary, they wanted the very beautiful thoughts attained by great men of deep devotion not to be ridiculed by those who are reluctant to exert themselves vigorously in any literary pursuit unless it is lucrative; or if they are stimulated to the nonacquisitive study of philosophy by the exhortation and example of others, yet because of their dullness of mind they play the same part among philosophers as drones among bees. When I weighed these considerations, the scorn which I had reason to fear on account of the novelty and unconventionality of my opinion almost induced me to abandon completely the work which I had undertaken.

From *Copernicus and the Scientific Revolution*, Edward Rosen, Robert E. Krieger Publishing Company.

But while I hesitated for a long time and even resisted, my friends drew me back. Foremost among them was the cardinal of Capua, Nicholas Schönberg, renowned in every field of learning. Next to him was a man who loves me dearly, Tiedemann Giese, bishop of Chelmno, a close student of sacred letters as well as of all good literature. For he repeatedly encouraged me and, sometimes adding reproaches, urgently requested me to publish this volume and finally permit it to appear after being buried among my papers and lying concealed not merely until the ninth year but by now the fourth period of nine years. The same conduct was recommended to me by not a few other very eminent scholars. They exhorted me no longer to refuse, on account of the fear which I felt, to make my work available for the general use of students of astronomy. The crazier my doctrine of the earth's motion now appeared to most people, the argument ran, so much the more admiration and thanks would it gain after they saw the publication of my writings dispel the fog of absurdity by most luminous proofs. Influenced therefore by these persuasive men and by this hope, in the end I allowed my friends to bring out an edition of the volume, as they had long besought me to do.

Critical Thinking Questions

1. In your own words, what reasons does Copernicus give for delaying publication? Why does he finally decide to publish the volume?

2. Drawing more generally on the document, and making some inferences, characterize the apparent intellectual atmosphere of the day.

Francis Bacon and the Method of Science

(1620)

The British statesman and philosopher Francis Bacon (1561–1626) contributed significantly to establishing the methods of modern science. Like his contemporary, Rene Descartes, he advocated a fresh start and new methods of inquiry. The following "aphorisms" are from his Novum Organum *of 1620.*

I

Man, being the servant and interpreter of Nature, can do and understand so much and so much only as he has observed in fact or in thought of the course of nature. Beyond this he neither knows anything nor can do anything.

II

Neither the naked hand nor the understanding left to itself can effect much. It is by instruments and helps that the work is done, which are as much wanted for the understanding as for the hand. And as the instruments of the hand either give motion or guide it, so the instruments of the mind supply either suggestions for the understanding or cautions.

III

Human knowledge and human power meet in one; for where the cause is not known the effect cannot be produced. Nature to be commanded must be obeyed; and that which in contemplation is as the cause is in operation as the rule.

V

The study of nature with a view to works is engaged in by the mechanic, the mathematician, the physician, the alchemist, and the magician; but by all (as things now are) with slight endeavor and scanty success.

VI

It would be an unsound fancy and self-contradictory to expect that things which have never yet been done can be done except by means which have never yet been tried.

VIII

Moreover, the works already known are due to chance and experiment rather than to sciences; for the sciences we now possess are merely systems for the nice ordering and setting forth of things already invented, not methods of invention or directions for new works.

XII

The logic now in use serves rather to fix and give stability to the errors which have their foundation in commonly received notions than to help the search after truth. So it does more harm than good.

From *The New Organon and Relations Writings* by Francis Bacon, The Bobbs-Merrill Company, Inc.

XIX

There are and can be only two ways of searching into and discovering truth. The one flies from the senses and particulars to the most general axioms, and from these principles, the truth of which it takes for settled and immovable, proceeds to judgment and to the discovery of middle axioms. And this way is now in fashion. The other derives axioms from the senses and particulars, rising by a gradual and unbroken ascent, so that it arrives at the most general axioms last of all. This is the true way, but as yet untried.

XX

The understanding left to itself takes the same course (namely, the former) which it takes in accordance with logical order. For the mind longs to spring up to positions of higher generality, that it may find rest there, and so after a little while wearies of experiment. But this evil is increased by logic, because of the order and solemnity of its disputations.

XXI

The understanding left to itself, in a sober, patient, and grave mind, especially if it be not hindered by received doctrines, tries a little that other way, which is the right one, but with little progress, since the understanding, unless directed and assisted, is a thing unequal, and quite unfit to contend with the obscurity of things.

XXII

Both ways set out from the senses and particulars, and rest in the highest generalities; but the difference between them is infinite. For the one just glances at experiment and particulars in passing, the other dwells duly and orderly among them. The one, again, begins at once by establishing certain abstract and useless generalities, the other rises by gradual steps to that which is prior and better known in the order of nature.

XXVI

The conclusions of human reason as ordinarily applied in matters of nature, I call for the sake of distinction *Anticipations of Nature* (as a thing rash or premature). That reason which is elicited from facts by a just and methodical process, I call *Interpretation of Nature*.

XXX

Though all the wits of all the ages should meet together and combine and transmit their labors, yet will no great progress ever be made in science by means of anticipations; because radical errors in the first concoction of the mind are not to be cured by the excellence of functions and subsequent remedies.

XXXVI

One method of delivery alone remains to us which is simply this: we must lead men to the particulars themselves, and their series and order; while men on their side must force themselves for a while to lay their notions by and begin to familiarize themselves with facts.

Critical Thinking Questions

1. How does Bacon believe that truth should be discovered? Which aphorism(s) discuss or advocate an "inductive" approach to learning?

2. How does Bacon feel about current methods of learning? Which aphorism(s) discuss his opinions on current learning techniques?

3. Pick any one aphorism and translate it as best you can into clear, modern English, preserving Bacon's original sense.

Voltaire, A Treatise on Toleration
(1763)

Francois-Marie Arouet (1694–1778), known by his pen name Voltaire, was one of the most influential philosophes of the Enlightenment. Voltaire wrote on many political and social issues, but he is probably most famous for his attacks on traditional religion, especially Christianity, and for advocating religious toleration. Due to censorship laws and laws against criticizing the established Catholic Church in France, Voltaire was frequently imprisoned and temporarily exiled for his controversial beliefs. In the following excerpt, Voltaire uses his famous wit and satirical style to articulate the dangers of religious and cultural intolerance.

Whether It Is Useful to Maintain People in Their Superstition

Such is the feebleness of humanity, such is its perversity, that doubtless it is better for it to be subject to all possible superstitions, as long as they are not murderous, than to live without religion. Man always needs to rein, and even if it might be ridiculous to sacrifice to fauns, or sylvans, or naiads, (1) it is much more reasonable and more useful to venerate these fantastic images of the Divine than to sink into atheism. An atheist who is rational, violent, and powerful, would be as great a pestilence as a blood-mad, superstitious man.

When men do not have healthy notions of the Divinity, false ideas supplant them, just as in bad times one uses counterfeit money when there is no good money. The pagan feared to commit any crime, out of fear of punishment by his false gods; the Malabarian fears to be punished by his pagoda. Wherever there is a settled society, religion is necessary; the laws cover manifest crimes, and religion covers secret crimes.

But whenever human faith comes to embrace a pure and holy religion, superstition not only becomes useless, but very dangerous. We should not seek to nourish ourselves on acorns when God gives us bread.

Superstition is to religion what astrology is to astronomy: the foolish daughter of a very wise mother. These two daughters, superstition and astrology, have subjugated the world for a long time.

When, in our ages of barbarity, scarcely two feudal lords owned between them a single New Testament, it might be pardonable to offer fables to the vulgar, that is, to these feudal lords, to their imbecile wives, and to their brutish vassals; they were led to believe that Saint Christopher carried the infant Jesus from one side of a river to the other; they were fed stories about sorcerers and their spiritual possessions; they easily imagined that Saint Genou (2) would cure the gout, and that Saint Claire (3) would cure eye problems. The children believed in the werewolf, and the fathers in the rope girdle of Saint Francis. The number of relics (4) was innumerable.

The sediment of these superstitions still survived among the people, even at that time that religion was purified. We know that when Monsieur de Noailles, the Bishop of Châlons, removed and threw into the fire the false relic of the holy navel of Jesus Christ, then the entire village of Châlons began proceedings against him; however, he had as much courage as he had piety, and he succeeded in making the Champenois believe that they could adore Jesus Christ in spirit and truth, without having his navel in the church.

Those we call Jansenists (5) contributed greatly to rooting out gradually from the spirit of the nation the greater part of the false ideas which dishonored the Christian religion. People ceased to believe that it was sufficient to recite a prayer to the Virgin Mary for thirty days so that they could do what they wish and sin with impunity the rest of the year.

Finally the bourgeoisie began to realize that it was not Saint Geneviève who gave or witheld rain, but that it was God Himself who disposed of the elements. The monks were astonished that their saints did not bring about miracles any longer; and if the writers of The Life of Saint Francis Xavier returned to the world, they would not dare to write that the saint revived nine corpses, that he was in two places, on the sea and on land, at the same time, and his crucifix fell into the sea and was restored to him by a crab.

It is the same with excommunications. Our historians tells us that when King Robert was excommunicated by Pope Gregory V, for marrying his godmother, the princess Bertha, his domestic servants threw the meats to be served to the king right out the window, and Queen Bertha gave birth to a goose in punishment for the incestuous marriage. One could seriously doubt that in this day and age the servants of the king of France, if he were excommunicated, would throw his dinner out the window, or that the queen would give birth to a goose.

There are still a few convulsive fanatics (6) in remote corners of the suburbs; but this disease only attacks the most vile population. Each day reason penetrates further into France, into the shops of merchants as well as the mansions of lords. We must cultivate the fruits of this reason, especially since it is impossible to check its advance. One cannot govern France, after it has been enlightened by Pascal, Nicole, Arnauld, Bossuiet, Descartes, Gassendi, Bayle, Fontenelle, and the others, as it as been governed in the times of Garasse and Menot.

If the masters of errors, and I'm speaking here of the grand masters, so long paid and honored for abusing the human species, ordered us today to believe that the seed must die in order to germinate; that the world is immovable on its foundations, that it does not orbit around the sun; that the tides are not a natural effect of gravitation; that the rainbow is not formed by the refraction and the reflection of rays of light, and so on, and they based their ordinances on passages poorly understood from the Holy Bible, how would educated men regard these men? Would the term "beasts" seem too strong? And if these wise masters used force and persecution to enforce their insolent stupidity, would the term "wild beasts" seem too extreme?

The more the superstitions of monks are despised, the more the bishops are respected and the priests listened to; while they do no good, these monkish superstitions from over the mountains (7) do a great deal of harm. But of all these superstitions, is not the most dangerous that of hating your neighbor for his opinions? And is it not evident that it would be much more reasonable to worship the Holy Navel, the Holy Foreskin, or the milk or the robe of the Virgin Mary, (8) than to detest the persecute your brother?

On Universal Tolerance

It does not require great art, or magnificently trained eloquence, to prove that Christians should tolerate each other. I, however, am going further: I say that we should regard all men as our brothers. What? The Turk my brother? The Chinaman my brother? The Jew? The Siam? Yes, without doubt; are we not all children of the same father and creatures of the same God?

But these people despise us; they treat us as idolaters! Very well! I will tell them that they are grievously wrong. It seems to me that I would at least astonish the proud, dogmatic Islam imam or Buddhist priest, if I spoke to them as follows:

"This little globe, which is but a point, rolls through space, as do many other globes; we are lost in the immensity of the universe. Man, only five feet high, is assuredly only a small thing in creation. One of these imperceptible beings says to another one of his neighbors, in Arabia or South Africa: 'Listen to me, because God of all these worlds has enlightened me: there are nine hundred million little ants like us on the earth, but my ant-hole is the only one dear to God; all the other are cast off by Him for eternity; mine alone will be happy, and all the others will be eternally damned.'"

They would then interrupt me, and ask which fool blabbed all this nonsense. I would be obliged to answer. "You, yourselves." I would then endeavor to calm them, which would be very difficult.

I would then speak with the Christians, and I would dare to say, for example, to a Dominican Inquisitor of the Faith: (9) "My brother, you know that each province of Italy has their own dialect, and that people do not speak at Venice or Bergamo the same way they speak at Florence. The Academy of Crusca near Florence has fixed the language; its dictionary is a rule which one dare not depart from, and the Grammar of Buonmattei is an infallible guide that one must follow. But do you believe that the consul of the Academy, or Buonmattei in his absence, could in conscience cut the tongues out of all the Venetians and all the Bergamese who persist in speaking their dialect?"

The inquisitor responds, "There is a difference between your example and our practice. For us, it is a matter of the health of your soul. It is for your good that the director of the Inquisition ordains that you be seized on the testimony of a single person, however infamous or criminal that person might be; that you will have no advocate to defend you; that the name of your accuser will not even be known by you; that the inquisitor can promise you mercy, and immediately condemn you; that five different tortures will be applied to you, and then you will be flogged, or sent to the galleys, or ceremoniously burned. Father Ivonet, Doctor Cuchalon, Zanchinus, Campegius, Roias, Felynus, Gomarus, Diabarus, Gemelinus, are explicit on this point, and this pious practice cannot suffer any contradiction."

I would take the liberty to respond, "My brother, perhaps you are reasonable; I am convinced that you wish to do me good; but could I not be saved without all that?"

It is true that these absurd horrors do not stain the face of the earth day; but they are frequent, and they could easily fill a volume much greater than the gospels which condemn them. (10) Not only is it extremely cruel to persecute in this brief life those who do not think the way we do, but I do not know if it might be too presumptuous to declare their eternal damnation. It seems to me that it does not pertain to the atoms of the moment, such as we are, to anticipate the decrees of the Creator.

End Notes

1. Ancient Greek demigods.
2. His name means "knee" in French.
3. Her name suggests light.
4. Physical remains of saints, either their body parts, clothing, or any other physical object associated with them; these relics were supposed to display remarkable curative and other magical properties.
5. Reformers who agreed in many ways with Protestant ideas.
6. Ecstatics who fell into religious fits.
7. Rome.
8. These are all relics actually venerated in his time.
9. The Dominicans ran the notorious Inquisition which tortured and condemned to death people who departed from orthodox Catholicism.
10. Note how he slips in this comment, arguing that the Inquisition itself is contrary to the teachings of Christ.

Critical Thinking Questions

1. What reasons does Voltaire give for showing tolerance to one another?

2. How does Voltaire feel about superstition? Is it useful or not, for example?

3. In your own words, summarize the main point of Voltaire's argument in his hypothetical conversation with the Dominican Inquisitor. How does the Inquisitor justify his actions?

4. What does Voltaire suggest will happen to those who are intolerant? Why?

Adam Smith's Free-Market Capitalism
(1776)

The Scottish-born economist Adam Smith is recognized as the father of free-market capitalism. His theories were published in a 1776 masterpiece, The Wealth of Nations, *which remains highly influential to this day, especially in the United States. In the following excerpts, Smith discusses the key market mechanisms of supply and demand.*

The market price of every particular commodity is regulated by the proportion between the quantity which is actually brought to market, and the demand of those who are willing to pay the natural price of the commodity, or the whole value of the rent, labour, and profit, which must be paid in order to bring it thither. Such people may be called the effectual demanders, and their demand the effectual demand; since it may be sufficient to effectuate the bringing of the commodity to market. It is different from the absolute demand. A very poor man may be said in some sense to have a demand for a coach and six; he might like to have it; but his demand is not an effectual demand, as the commodity can never be brought to market in order to satisfy it.

When the quantity of any commodity which is brought to market falls short of the effectual demand, all those who are willing to pay the whole value of the rent, wages, and profit, which must be paid in order to bring it thither, cannot be supplied with the quantity which they want. Rather than want it altogether, some of them will be willing to give more. A competition will immediately begin among them, and the market price will rise more or less above the natural price, according as either the greatness of the deficiency, or the wealth and wanton luxury of the competitors, happen to animate more or less the eagerness of the competition.

Among competitors of equal wealth and luxury the same deficiency will generally occasion a more or less eager competition, according as the acquisition of the commodity happens to be of more or less importance to them. Hence the exorbitant price of the necessaries of life during the blockade of a town or in a famine.

When the quantity brought to market exceeds the effectual demand, it cannot be all sold to those who are willing to pay the whole value of the rent, wages and profit, which must be paid in order to bring it thither. Some part must be sold to those who are willing to pay less, and the low price which they give for it must reduce the price of the whole. The market price will sink more or less below the natural price, according as the greatness of the excess increases more or less the competition of the sellers, or according as it happens to be more or less important to them to get immediately rid of the commodity. The same excess in the importation of perishable, will occasion a much greater competition than in that of durable commodities; in the importation of oranges, for example, than in that of old iron.

When the quantity brought to market is just sufficient to supply the effectual demand and no more, the market price naturally comes to be either exactly, or as nearly as can be judged of, the same

---

From *The Wealth of Nations* by Adam Smith, The Modern Library.

with the natural price. The whole quantity upon hand can be disposed of for this price, and cannot be disposed of for more. The competition of the different dealers obliges them all to accept of this price, but does not oblige them to accept of less.

The quantity of every commodity brought to market naturally suits itself to the effectual demand. It is the interest of all those who employ their land, labour, or stock, in bringing any commodity to market, that the quantity never should exceed the effectual demand; and it is the interest of all other people that it never should fall short of that demand....

The produce of industry is what it adds to the subject or materials upon which it is employed. In proportion as the value of this produce is great or small, so will likewise be the profits of the employer. But it is only for the sake of profit that any man employs capital in the support of industry; and he will always, therefore, endeavour to employ it in the support of that industry of which the produce is likely to be of the greatest value, or to exchange for the greatest quantity either of money or of other goods.

But the annual revenue of every society is always precisely equal to the exchangeable value of the whole annual produce of its industry, or rather is precisely the same thing with that exchangeable value. As every individual, therefore, endeavours as much as he can both to employ his capital in the support of domestic industry, and so to direct that industry that its produce may be of the greatest value; every individual necessarily labours to render the annual revenue of the society as great as he can. He generally, indeed, neither intends to promote the public interest, nor knows how much he is promoting it. By preferring the support of domestic to that of foreign industry, he intends only his own security; and by directing that industry in such a manner as its produce may be of the greatest value, he intends only his own gain, and he is in this, as in many other cases, led by an invisible hand to promote an end which was no part of his intention. Nor is it always, the worse for the society that it was no part of it. By pursuing his own interest he frequently promotes that of the society more effectually than when he really intends to promote it. I have never known much good done by those who affected to trade for the public good. It is an affectation, indeed, not very common among merchants, and very few words need be employed in dissuading them from it.

What is the species of domestic industry which his capital can employ, and of which the produce is likely to be of the greatest value, every individual, it is evident, can, in his local situation, judge much better than any statesman or lawgiver can do for him. The statesman, who should attempt to direct private people in what manner they ought to employ their capitals, would not only load himself with a most unnecessary attention, but assume an authority which could safely be trusted, not only to no single person, but to no council or senate whatever, and which would nowhere be so dangerous as in the hands of a man who had folly and presumption enough to fancy himself fit to exercise it.

Critical Thinking Questions

1. What is the difference between "effectual demand" and "absolute demand"? Between what Smith defines as the "natural price" of an item and its "market price"?

2. How does the principle of supply and demand regulate the market?

3. What is the "invisible hand"? What does Smith mean by this term?

The French Revolution

Declaration of the Rights of Man and of the Citizen (1789)

Declaration of the Rights of Woman and of the Citizen (1791)

Declaration of the Rights of Man and of the Citizen
(1789)

This document was approved by the National Assembly of France on August 26, 1789. Like the American Declaration of Independence, *it draws heavily on the ideals of the Enlightenment and identifies and guarantees certain "natural" or "inalienable" universal rights.*

Preamble

The representatives of the French people, organized as a national assembly, considering that ignorance, neglect, and scorn of the rights of man are the sole causes of public misfortunes and of corruption of governments, have resolved to display in a solemn declaration the natural, inalienable, and sacred rights of man, so that this declaration, constantly in the presence of all members of society, will continually remind them of their rights and their duties; so that the acts of the legislative power and those of the executive power, being subject at any time to comparison with the purpose of any political institution, will be better respected; so that the demands of the citizens, based henceforth on simple and incontestable principles, will always contribute to the maintenance of the constitution and the happiness of all.

Consequently, the National Assembly recognizes and declares, in the presence and under the auspices of the Supreme Being, the following rights of man and citizen:

Article 1. Men are born and remain free and equal in rights; social distinctions can be established only for the common benefit.

2. The aim of every political association is the conservation of the natural and imprescriptible rights of man; these rights are liberty, property, security, and resistance to oppression.

3. The source of all sovereignty is located in essence in the nation; no body, no individual can exercise authority which does not emanate from it expressly.

4. Liberty consists in being able to do anything that does not harm another person. Thus the exercise of the natural rights of each man has no limits except those which assure to the other members of society the enjoyment of these same rights; these limits can be determined only by law.

5. The law has the right to forbid only those actions harmful to society. All that is not forbidden by the law cannot be hindered, and no one can be forced to do what it does not order.

6. The law is the expression of the general will; all citizens have the right to concur personally or through their representatives in its formation; it must be the same for all, whether it protects or punishes. All citizens being equal in its eyes are equally admissible to all honors, positions, and public

---

From *The French Revolution* translated by Paul H. Beik. Copyright © 1971 by Walker and Company. Reprinted by permission.

employments, according to their capabilities and without other distinctions than those of their virtues and talents.

7. No man can be accused, arrested, or detained except in cases determined by the law, and according to the forms which it has prescribed. Those who solicit, draw up, execute, or have executed arbitrary orders must be punished; but any citizen summoned or seized by virtue of the law must obey instantly; he renders himself culpable by resisting.

8. The law must establish only penalties that are strictly and clearly necessary, and no one can be punished except in virtue of a law established and published prior to the offense and legally applied.

9. Every man being presumed innocent until he has been declared guilty, if it is judged indispensable to arrest him, all severity that is not necessary for making sure of his person must be severely repressed by the law.

10. No one may be disturbed because of his opinions, even religious, provided that their public demonstration does not disturb the public order established by law.

11. The free communication of thoughts and opinions is one of the most precious rights of man: every citizen can therefore freely speak, write, and print: he is answerable for abuses of this liberty in cases determined by the law.

12. The guaranteeing of the rights of man and citizen necessitates a public force; this force is therefore instituted for the advantage of all, and not for the private use of those to whom it is entrusted.

13. For the maintenance of the public force, and for the expenses of administration, a tax supported in common is indispensable; it must be assessed on all citizens in proportion to their capacities to pay.

14. Citizens have the right to determine for themselves or through their representatives the need for taxation of the public, to consent to it freely, to investigate its use, and to determine its rate, basis, collection, and duration.

15. Society has the right to demand an accounting of his administration from every public agent.

16. Any society in which guarantees of rights are not assured nor the separation of powers determined has no constitution.

17. Property being an inviolable and sacred right, no one may be deprived of it unless public necessity, legally determined, clearly requires such action, and then only on condition of a just and prior indemnity.

Critical Thinking Questions

1. Where does sovereignty lie according to the National Assembly?

2. What rights do French citizens have under this document?

3. Do clauses 10–11 establish freedom of religion or not? Why or why not?

4. Choose one or two sentences or short passages you think best encapsulate the overall spirit of the document. Briefly explain your choices.

Declaration of the Rights of Woman and of the Citizen
(1791)

The following document was written by Olympe de Gouge, a butcher's daughter and women's rights advocate. Her efforts on behalf of her sex were not appreciated by the National Convention, which convicted her of treason. She was guillotined in late 1793.

Declaration of the Rights of Woman and Citizen,
To be decreed by the National Assembly in its last meetings or in those of the next legislature.

Preamble

The mothers, daughters, and sisters, representatives of the nation, demand to be constituted a national assembly. Considering that ignorance, disregard of or contempt for the rights of women are the only causes of public misfortune and of governmental corruption, they have resolved to set forth in a solemn declaration, the natural, inalienable and sacred rights of woman; to the end that this declaration, constantly held up to all members of society, may always remind them of their rights and duties; to the end that the acts based on women's power and those based on the power of men, being constantly measured against the goal of all political institutions, may be more respected; and so that the demands of female citizens, henceforth founded on simple and indisputable principles, may ever uphold the constitution and good morals, and may contribute to the happiness of all.

Consequently, the sex that is superior in beauty as well as in courage of maternal suffering, recognizes and declares, in the presence and under the auspices of the Supreme Being, the following rights of woman and citizen....

Postamble

Woman, wake up! The tocsin of reason is sounding throughout the Universe; know your rights. The powerful empire of nature is no longer surrounded by prejudices, fanaticism, superstition and lies. The torch of truth has dispelled all the clouds of stupidity and usurpation. Man enslaved has multiplied his forces; he has had recourse to yours in order to break his own chains. Having become free, he has become unjust toward his mate. Oh Women! Women! when will you cease to be blind? What advantages have you gained in the Revolution? A more marked scorn, a more signal disdain. During centuries of corruption, you reigned only over the weakness of men. Your empire is destroyed; what then remains for you? The proof of man's injustice. The claim of your patrimony founded on the wise decrees of nature—what have you to fear from such a splendid enterprise? The good word of the legislator at the marriage of Canaan? Do you not fear that our French legislators, who are correcting this morality, which was for such a long time appended to the realm of politics but is no longer fashionable, will again say to you, "Women, what do

---

From Susan Groag Bell and Karen M. Offen, *Women, the Family & Freedom*. Copyright © 1983 by the Board of Trustees of the Leland Stanford Jr. University. All rights reserved. Used with the permission of Stanford University Press, www.sup.org.

we have in common with you?" You must answer, "Everything!" If, in their weakness, they are obstinate in drawing this conclusion contrary to their principles, you must courageously invoke the force of reason against their vain pretensions of superiority. Unite yourselves under the banner of philosophy; deploy all the energy of your character, and soon you will see these prideful ones, your adoring servants, no longer grovelling at your feet but proud to share with you the treasures of the Supreme Being. Whatever the obstacles that are put in your way, it is in your power to overturn them; you have only to will it. Let us turn now to the frightful picture of what you have been in society; and since there is currently a question of national education, let us see if our wise legislators will think wisely about the education of women.

Women have done more evil than good. They have had their share in coercion and double-dealings. When forcibly abused, they have countered with stratagems; they have had recourse to all the resources of their charms, and the most blameless among them has not hesitated to use them. They have used poison and irons; they have commanded crime and virtue alike. For centuries, the government of France in particular has depended on the nocturnal administration of women; the cabinet had no secrets from their indiscretion: embassy, military command, ministry, presidency, pontificate, cardinalate—one might say everything profane and sacred subject to the foolishness of man has been subordinated to the greed and ambition of the female sex, which was formerly contemptible and respected but, since the revolution, is respectable and yet contemptible.

What could I not say about this paradox! I have only a moment for offering a few remarks, but this moment will attract the attention of the most remote posterity. Under the Old Regime, all were vicious, all were guilty; but could one not perceive the improvement of things, even in the substance of vice? A woman needed only to be beautiful or lovable; when she possessed these two advantages, she saw a hundred fortunes at her feet. If she did not profit from this situation, she had either a bizarre character or a rare philosophy that led her to despise wealth; in such a case she was relegated to the status of a brainless person; the most indecent woman could make herself respected with enough gold; the buying and selling of women was a kind of industry taken for granted in the first rank of society, which, henceforth, will have no credit. If it did, the revolution would be lost, and under the new order we would remain ever corrupt. Still, can reason hide the fact that all other routes to fortune are closed to woman, whom man buys like a slave on the African coast? The difference is great, as we know. The slave commands the master; but if the master sets her free, without compensation, at an age when the slave has lost all her charms, what becomes of this unfortunate creature? A contemptible toy; even the doors of charity are closed to her; she is poor and old, they say; why didn't she know how to make her fortune? Other more touching examples suggest themselves to reason. A young person without experience, seduced by a man she loves, will abandon her parents to follow him; the ungrateful fellow will leave her after a few years, and the older she has grown with him, the more inhuman will his inconstancy be. If she has children, he will abandon her all the same. If he is rich, he will think himself exempt from sharing his fortune with his noble victims. If some commitment binds him to his duties, he will violate its power by using all legal loopholes. If he is married, other commitments lose their rights. What laws then remain to be made in order to destroy vice down to its very roots? One dealing with the sharing of fortunes between men and women, and another with public administration. It is clear that a woman born to a rich family gains a great deal from equal inheritance. But a woman born to a poor family of merit and virtue—what is her fate? Poverty and shame. If she does not excel in music or painting, she cannot be admitted to any public office, even though she might be quite capable. I wish only to give an overview of things. I will examine them more thoroughly in the new edition of my political works, with notes, which I propose to offer to the public in a few days.

I resume my text with regard to morals. Marriage is the tomb of confidence and love. A married woman can, with impunity, present bastards to her husband and the bastards with the fortune that does not belong to them. An unmarried woman has merely a slim right: ancient and inhuman laws have refused her the right to the name and property of the father of her children, and no new laws on this matter have been passed. If my attempt thus to give my sex an honorable and just stability is now considered a paradox on my part, an attempt at the impossible, I must leave to men yet to come the glory of discussing this matter; but meanwhile, one can pave the way through national education, the restoration of morals, and by conjugal contracts.

Critical Thinking Questions

1. Compare the first paragraph of this document with the first paragraph of the Declaration of the Rights of Man and of the Citizen. What can you say about de Gouge's technique or strategy and its likely effectiveness?

2. What rights does de Gouge advocate for women?

3. Speculate which idea or part of the document might have caused the most offense to the revolutionary National Convention. Justify your answer.

II. The Long Nineteenth Century

The First Industrial Revolution in Europe

Charles Dickens, Hard Times *(1854)*

Testimony for the Factory Act of 1833: Working Conditions in England

Charles Dickens, Hard Times
(1854)

The First Industrial Revolution, which began in Great Britain in the late eighteenth century, had a tremendous impact on Britain and on all later industrialized countries. Hard Times *by Charles Dickens is one of the best and most well-known literary critiques of early industrialism. The following segment contrasts the fictitious industrial city of Coketown with the surrounding countryside.*

It was a town of red brick, or of brick that would have been red if the smoke and ashes had allowed it; but as matters stood it was a town of unnatural red and black like the painted face of a savage. It was a town of machinery and tall chimneys, out of which interminable serpents of smoke trailed themselves for ever and ever, and never got uncoiled. It had a black canal in it, and a river that ran purple with ill-smelling dye, and vast piles of buildings full of windows where there was a rattling and a trembling all day long, and where the piston of the steam-engine worked monotonously up and down like the head of an elephant in a state of melancholy madness. It contained several large streets all very like one another, and many small streets still more like one another, inhabited by people equally like one another, who all went in and out at the same hours, with the same sound upon the same pavements, to do the same work, and to whom every day was the same as yesterday and tomorrow, and every year the counterpart of the last and the next....

In the hardest working part of Coketown; in the innermost fortifications of that ugly citadel, where Nature was as strongly bricked out as killing airs and gases were bricked in; at the heart of the labyrinth of narrow courts upon courts, and close streets upon streets, which had come into existence piecemeal, every piece in a violent hurry for some one man's purpose, and the whole an unnatural family, shouldering, and trampling, and pressing one another to death; in the last close nook of this great exhausted receiver, where the chimneys, for want of air to make a draught, were built in an immense variety of stunted and crooked shapes, as though every house put out a sign of the kind of people who might be expected to be born in it; among the multitude of Coketown, generically called 'the Hands,'—a race who would have found more favour with some people, if Providence had seen fit to make them only hands, or, like the lower creatures of the seashore, only hands and stomachs—lived a certain Stephen Blackpool, forty years of age....

As Coketown cast ashes not only on its own head but on the neighbourhood's too—after the manner of those pious persons who do penance for their own sins by putting other people into sackcloth—it was customary for those who now and then thirsted for a draught of pure air, which is not absolutely the most wicked among the vanities of life, to get a few miles away by the railroad, and then begin their walk, or their lounge in the fields....

Though the green landscape was blotted here and there with heaps of coal, it was green elsewhere, and there were trees to see, and there were larks

---

From *Hard Times* by Charles Dickens, 1854.

singing (though it was Sunday), and there were pleasant scents in the air, and all was over-arched by a bright blue sky. In the distance one way, Coketown showed as a black mist; in another distance hills began to rise; in a third, there was a faint change in the light of the horizon where it shone upon the far-off sea. Under their feet, the grass was fresh; beautiful shadows of branches flickered upon it, and speckled it; hedgerows were luxuriant; everything was at peace. Engines at pits' mouths, and lean old horses that had worn the circle of their daily labour into the ground, were alike quiet; wheels had ceased for a short space to turn; and the great wheel of earth seemed to revolve without the shocks and noises of another time.

Critical Thinking Questions

1. What aspect of life in Coketown does Dickens seem most critical of?

2. What does Dickens imply has been the effect of industrialization on the working-class of Coketown?

3. What kinds of industry can one infer must have existed in Coketown?

Testimony for the Factory Act of 1833: Working Conditions in England

In the early decades of industrialization, when there was little government regulation of industry, factory and mine workers suffered terrible abuses at the hands of exploitative employers who sought to make a profit in a competitive free market economy. By the early nineteenth century, the British Parliament finally began to investigate the abuses of factory labor, culminating in the passage of the Factory Act of 1833. The following excerpts, which were taken from testimony given before the British Parliament, offer different perspectives on factory labor: the first comes from a commission of medical examiners; the second from John Wright, a worker in a silk factory; and the third from William Harter, a silk manufacturer.

Testimony of the Commission of Medical Examiners

The account of the physical condition of the manufacturing population in the large towns in the North-eastern District of England is less favourable. It is of this district that the Commissioners state, "We have found undoubted instances of children five years old sent to work thirteen hours a day; and frequently of children nine, ten, and eleven consigned to labour for fourteen and fifteen hours." The effects ascertained by the Commissioners in many cases are, "deformity," and in still more "stunted growth, relaxed muscles, and slender conformation:" "twisting of the ends of the long bones, relaxation of the ligaments of the knees, ankles, and the like." "The representation that these effects are so common and universal as to enable some persons invariably to distinguish factory children from other children is, I have no hesitation in saying, an exaggerated and unfaithful picture of their general condition; at the same time it must be said, that the individual instances in which some one or other of those effects of severe labour are discernible are rather frequent than rare....

"Upon the whole, there remains no doubt upon my mind, that under the system pursued in many of the factories, the children of the labouring classes stand in need of, and ought to have, legislative protection against the conspiracy insensibly formed between their masters and parents, to tax them to a degree of toil beyond their strength.

"In conclusion, I think it has been clearly proved that children have been worked a most unreasonable and cruel length of time daily, and that even adults have been expected to do a certain quantity of labour which scarcely any human being is able to endure. I am of opinion no child under fourteen years of age should work in a factory of any description for more than eight hours a day. From fourteen upwards I would recommend that no individual should, under any circumstances, work more than twelve hours a day; although if practicable, as a physician, I would

---

From Commission for Inquiry into the Employment of Children in Factories, Second Report with Minutes of Evidence and Reports by the Medical Commissioners, Vol. V, Session 29 January–August 1833, (London: His Majesty's Printing Office, 1833).

prefer the limitation of ten hours, for all persons who earn their bread by their industry."

Testimony of John Wright

How long have you been employed in a silk-mill?—More than thirty years.

Did you enter it as a child?—Yes, betwixt five and six.

How many hours a day did you work then?—The same thirty years ago as now.

What are those hours?—Eleven hours per day and two over-hours; over-hours are working after six in the evening till eight. The regular hours are from six in the morning to six in the evening, and two others are two over-hours: about fifty years ago they began working over-hours....

Why, then, are those employed in them said to be in such a wretched condition?—In the first place, the great number of hands congregated together, in some rooms forty, in some fifty, in some sixty, and I have known some as many as 100, which must be injurious to both health and growing. In the second place, the privy is in the factory, which frequently emits an unwholesome smell; and it would be worth while to notice in the future erection of mills, that there be betwixt the privy door and the factory wall a kind of a lobby of cage-work. 3dly, The tediousness and the everlasting sameness in the first process preys much on the spirits, and makes the hands spiritless. 4thly, the extravagant number of hours a child is compelled to labour and confinement, which for one week is seventy-six hours.... 5thly, About six months in the year we are obliged to use either gas, candles, or lamps, for the longest portion of that time, nearly six hours a day, being obliged to work amid the smoke and soot of the same; and also a large portion of oil and grease is used in the mills.

What are the effects of the present system of labour?—From my earliest recollections, I have found the effects to be awfully detrimental to the well-being of the operative; I have observed frequently children carried to factories, unable to walk, and that entirely owing to excessive labour and confinement. The degradation of the workpeople baffles all description: frequently have two of my sisters been obliged to be assisted to the factory and home again, until by-and-by they could go no longer, being totally crippled in their legs. And in the next place, I remember some ten or twelve years ago working in one of the largest firms in Macclesfield, (Messrs. Baker and Pearson,) with about twenty-five men, where they were scarce one half fit for His Majesty's service. Those that are straight in their limbs are stunted in their growth; much inferior to their fathers in point of strength. 3dly, Through excessive labour and confinement there is often a total loss of appetite; a kind of languor steals over the whole frame—enters to the very core—saps the foundation of the best constitution—and lays our strength prostrate in the dust. In the 4th place, by protracted labour there is an alarming increase of cripples in various parts of this town, which has come under my own observation and knowledge....

Are all these cripples made in the silk factories?—Yes, they are, I believe....

Testimony of William Harter

What effect would it have on your manufacture to reduce the hours of labour to ten?—It would instantly much reduce the value of my mill and machinery, and consequently of far prejudice my manufacture.

How so?—They are calculated to produce a certain quantity of work in a given time. Every machine is valuable in proportion to the quantity of work which it will turn off in a given time. It is impossible that the machinery could produce as much work in ten hours as in twelve. If the tending of the machines were a laborious occupation, the difference in the quantity of work might not always be in exact proportion to the difference of working time; but in my mill, and silk-mills in general, the work requires the least imaginable labour; therefore it is perfectly impossible that the machines could produce as much work in ten hours as in twelve. The produce would vary in about the same ratio as the working time.

Critical Thinking Questions

1. What specific abuse of factory labor seems to be the major concern of this source?

2. According to John Wright, what were working conditions like in the silk factories?

3. What perspective does William Harter provide? How does he respond to the idea of reducing working hours for laborers?

4. What do the *Hard Times* excerpt and the Testimony for the Factory Act of 1833 suggest about the impact of industrialization on the quality of human life, at least in the early decades? Is this still the case today? Explain.

Culture & Ideologies in Nineteenth Century Europe

Marx and Engels, The Communist Manifesto *(1848)*

Edmund Burke, Reflections on the Revolution in France *(1790)*

John Stuart Mill, "On Liberty" (1859)

Giuseppe Mazzini on Nationalism (1852)

Simón de Bolívar Addresses the Congress of Angostura (1819)

Theodor Herzl and Zionism (1896)

Charles Darwin, The Descent of Man *(1871)*

Marx and Engels, The Communist Manifesto
(1848)

Karl Marx and Friedrich Engels are the founding fathers of so-called scientific socialism. Their pamphlet, The Communist Manifesto, *and other writings by Marx, were a primary inspiration for the 1917 Bolshevik Revolution in Russia, the Chinese Communist Revolution of 1949, and other great upheavals.*

I. Bourgeois and Proletarians

The history of all hitherto existing societies is the history of class struggles.

Freeman and slave, patrician and plebeian, lord and serf, guild-master and journeyman, in a word, oppressor and oppressed, stood in constant opposition to one another, carried on an uninterrupted, now hidden, now open fight, a fight that each time ended, either in a revolutionary re-constitution of society at large, or in common ruin of the contending classes.

In the earlier epochs of history, we find almost everywhere a complicated arrangement of society into various orders, a manifold gradation of social rank. In ancient Rome we have patricians, knights, plebeians, slaves; in the Middle Ages, feudal lords, vassals, guild-masters, journeymen, apprentices, serfs; in almost all of these classes, again, subordinate gradations.

The modern bourgeois society that has sprouted from the ruins of feudal society has not done away with clash antagonisms. It has but established new classes, new conditions of oppression, new forms of struggle in place of the old ones. Our epoch, the epoch of the bourgeoisie, possesses, however, this distinctive feature: it has simplified the class antagonisms: Society as a whole is more and more splitting up into two great hostile camps, into two great classes, directly facing each other: Bourgeoisie and Proletariat. . . .

Modern industry has established the world-market, for which the discovery of America paved the way. This market has given an immense development to commerce, to navigation, to communication by land. This development has, in its time, reacted on the extension of industry; and in proportion as industry, commerce, navigation, railways extended, in the same proportion the bourgeoisie developed, increased its capital, and pushed into the background every class handed down from the Middle Ages. . . .

Each step in the development of the bourgeoisie was accompanied by a corresponding political advance of that class. An oppressed class under the sway of the feudal nobility, an armed and self-governing association in the mediaeval commune; here independent urban republic (as in Italy and Germany), there taxable "third estate" of the monarchy (as in France), afterwards, in the period of manufacture proper, serving either the semi-feudal or the absolute monarchy as a counterpoise against the

---

From *Communist Manifesto*, by Karl Marx and Frederick Engels, 1888 English edition.

nobility, and, in fact, corner-stone of the great monarchies in general, the bourgeoisie has at last, since the establishment of Modern Industry and of the world-market, conquered for itself, in the modern representative State, exclusive political sway. The executive of the modern State is but a committee for managing the common affairs of the whole bourgeoisie. . . .

In proportion as the bourgeoisie, i.e., capital, is developed, in the same proportion is the proletariat, the modern working class, developed—a class of labourers, who live only so long as they find work, and who find work only so long as their labour increases capital. . . .

The proletariat goes through various stages of development. With its birth begins its struggle with the bourgeoisie. At first the contest is carried on by individual labourers, then by the workpeople of a factory, then by the operatives of one trade, in one locality, against the individual bourgeois who directly exploits them. They direct their attacks not against the bourgeois conditions of production, but against the instruments of production themselves; they destroy imported wares that compete with their labour, they smash to pieces machinery, they set factories ablaze, they seek to restore by force the vanished status of the workman of the Middle Ages.

At this stage the labourers still form an incoherent mass scattered over the whole country, and broken up by their mutual competition. If anywhere they unite to form more compact bodies, this is not yet the consequence of their own active union, but of the union of the bourgeoisie, which class, in order to attain its own political ends, is compelled to set the whole proletariat in motion, and is moreover yet, for a time, able to do so. At this stage therefore, the proletarians do not fight their enemies, but the enemies of their enemies, the remnants of absolute monarchy, the landowners, the non-industrial bourgeois, the petty bourgeoisie. Thus the whole historical movement is concentrated in the hands of the bourgeoisie; every victory so obtained is a victory for the bourgeoisie.

But with the development of industry the proletariat not only increases in number; it becomes concentrated in greater masses, its strength grows, and it feels that strength more. The various interests and conditions of life within the ranks of the proletariat are more and more equalised, in proportion as machinery obliterates all distinctions of labour, and nearly everywhere reduces wages to the same low level. The growing competition among the bourgeois, and the resulting commercial crises, make the wages of the workers ever more fluctuating. The unceasing improvement of machinery, ever more rapidly developing, makes their livelihood more and more precarious; the collisions between individual workmen and individual bourgeois take more and more the character of collisions between two classes. Thereupon the workers begin to form combinations (Trades unions) against the bourgeois; they club together in order to keep up the rate of wages; they found permanent associations in order to make provision beforehand for theses occasional revolts. Here and there the contest breaks out into riots.

Altogether collisions between the classes of the old society further, in many ways, the course of development of the proletariat. The bourgeoisie finds itself involved in a constant battle. At first with the aristocracy; later on, with those portions of the bourgeoisie itself, whose interests have become antagonistic to the progress of industry; at all times, with the bourgeoisie of foreign countries. In all these battles it sees itself compelled to appeal to the proletariat, to ask for its help, and thus, to drag it into the political arena. The bourgeoisie itself, therefore, supplies the proletariat with its own instruments of political and general education, in other words, it furnishes the proletariat with weapons for fighting the bourgeoisie.

Further, as we have already seen, entire sections of the ruling classes are, by the advance of industry, precipitated into the proletariat, or are at least threatened in their conditions of existence. These also supply the proletariat with fresh elements of enlightenment and progress.

Finally, in times when the class struggle nears the decisive hour, the process of dissolution going on within the ruling class, in fact within the whole range of society, assumes such a violent, glaring character, that a small section of the ruling class cuts itself adrift, and joins the revolutionary class, the class that holds the future in its hands. Just as, therefore, at an earlier period, a section of the nobility went over to the bourgeoisie, so now a portion of the bourgeoisie goes over to the proletariat, and in particular, a portion of the bourgeois ideologists, who have raised themselves to the level of comprehending theoretically the historical movement as a whole.

Of all the classes that stand face to face with the bourgeoisie today, the proletariat alone is a really revolutionary class. The other classes decay and finally disappear in the face of Modern Industry; the proletariat is its special and essential product. The lower middle class, the small manufacturer, the shopkeeper, the artisan, the peasant, all these fight against the bourgeoisie, to save from extinction their existence as fractions of the middle class. They are therefore not revolutionary, but conservative. Nay more, they are reactionary, for they try to roll back the wheel of history....

All previous historical movements were movements of minorities, or in the interests of minorities. The proletarian movement is the self-conscious, independent movement of the immense majority, in the interests of the immense majority. The proletariat, the lowest stratum of our present society, cannot stir, cannot raise itself up, without the whole superincumbent strata of official society being sprung into the air....

Hitherto, every form of society has been based, as we have already seen, on the antagonism of oppressing and oppressed class. But in order to oppress a class, certain conditions must be assured to it under which it can, at least, continue its slavish existence. The serf, in the period of serfdom, raised himself to membership in the commune, just as the petty bourgeois, under the yoke of feudal absolutism, managed to develop into a bourgeois. The modern laborer, on the contrary, instead of rising with the progress of industry, sinks deeper and deeper below the conditions of existence of his own class. He becomes a pauper, and pauperism develops more rapidly than population and wealth. And here it becomes evident, that the bourgeoisie is unfit any longer to be the ruling class in society, and to impose its conditions of existence upon society as an overriding law. It is unfit to rule because it is incompetent to assure an existence to its slave within his slavery, because it cannot help letting him sink into such a state, that it has to feed him, instead of being fed by him. Society can no longer live under this bourgeoisie, in other words, its existence is no longer compatible with society.

The essential condition for the existence, and for the sway of the bourgeois class, is the formation and augmentation of capital; the condition for capital is wage-labour. Wage-labour rests exclusively on competition between the laborers. The advance of industry, whose involuntary promoter is the bourgeoisie, replaces the isolation of the labourers, due to competition, by their revolutionary combination, due to association. The development of Modern Industry, therefore, cuts from under its feet the very foundation on which the bourgeoisie produces and appropriates products. What the bourgeoisie, therefore, produces, above all, is its own grave-diggers. Its fall and victory of the proletariat are equally inevitable.

II. Proletarians and Communists

The immediate aim of the Communist is the same as that of all the other proletarian parties: formation of the proletariat into a class, overthrow of the bourgeois supremacy, conquest of political power by the proletariat....

The distinguishing feature of Communism is not the abolition of property generally, but the abolition of bourgeois property. But modern bourgeois private property is the final and most complete expression of the system of producing and appropriating products, that is based on class antagonisms, on the exploitation of the many by the few.

In this sense, the theory of the Communists may be summed up in the single sentence: Abolition of private property....

We communists have been reproached with the desire of abolishing the right of personally acquiring property as the fruit of a man's own labour, which property is alleged to be the groundwork of all personal freedom, activity and independence.

Hard-won, self-acquired, self-earned property! Do you mean property of the petty artisan and of the small peasant, a form of property that preceded the bourgeois form? There is no need to abolish that; the development of industry has to a great extent already destroyed it, and is still destroying it daily.

Or do you mean the modern bourgeois private property?

But does wage labor create any property for the laborer? Not a bit. It creates capital, i.e., that kind of property which exploits wage labor, and which cannot increase except upon conditions of begetting a new supply of wage labor for fresh exploitation....

You are horrified at our intending to do away with private property. But in your existing society, private property is already done away with for nine-tenths of the population; its existence for the few is solely due to its non-existence in the hands of those none-tenths. You reproach us, therefore, with intending to do away with a form of property, the necessary condition for whose existence is the non-existence of any property for the immense majority of society....

The Communists are further reproached with desiring to abolish countries and nationality.

The working men have no country. We cannot take from them what they have not got. Since the proletariat must first of all acquire political supremacy, must rise to be the leading class of the nation, must constitute itself the nation, it is, so far, itself national, though not in the bourgeois sense of the word.

National differences and antagonisms between peoples are daily more and more vanishing, owing to the development of the bourgeoisie, to freedom of commerce, to the world-market, to uniformity in the mode of production and in the conditions of life corresponding thereto.

The supremacy of the proletariat will cause them to vanish still faster. United action, of the leading civilised countries at least, is one of the first conditions for the emancipation of the proletariat.

In proportion as the exploitation of one individual by another will also be put an end to, the exploitation of one nation by another will also be put an end to. In proportion as the antagonism between classes within the nation vanishes, the hostility of one nation to another will come to an end.

The charges against Communism made from a religious, a philosophical, and, generally, from an ideological standpoint, are not deserving of serious examination....

What else does the history of ideas prove, than that intellectual production changes its character in proportion as material production is changed? The ruling ideas of each age have ever been the ideas of its ruling class....

"Undoubtedly," it will be said, "religious, moral, philosophical and juridical ideas have been modified in the course of historical development. But religion, morality philosophy, political science, and law, constantly survived this change."

"There are, besides, eternal truths, such as Freedom, Justice, etc. that are common to all states of society. But Communism abolished eternal truths, it abolishes all religion, and all morality, instead of constituting them on a new basis; it therefore acts in contradiction to all past historical experience."

What does this accusation reduce itself to? The history of all past society has consisted in the development of class antagonisms, antagonisms that assumed different forms at different epochs.

But whatever form they may have taken, one fact is common to all past ages, viz., the exploitation of one part of society by the other. No wonder, then, that the social consciousness of past ages, despite all the multiplicity and variety it displays, moves within certain common forms, or general ideas, which cannot completely vanish except with the total disappearance of class antagonisms.

The Communist revolution is the most radical rupture with traditional property relations; no wonder that its development involves the most radical rupture with traditional ideas....

The Communists disdain to conceal their views and aims. They openly declare that their ends can be attained only by the forcible overthrow of the existing social conditions. Let the ruling classes tremble at a Communistic revolution. The proletarians have nothing to lose but their chains. They have a world to win.

Working men of all countries, unite!

Critical Thinking Questions

1. In the Marxist view, what is the main source of conflict throughout history? What groups are currently in conflict with one another?

2. What are the major stages in the class struggle as the proletariat develops?

3. What do Marx and Engels feel makes the proletariat unlike any other class that has ever existed?

4. What is the goal of the Communist party? How will this end be achieved?

5. What are some of the major features of communist society, according to the Manifesto? Why might these characteristics be frightening to certain classes within society?

6. What will happen to the nation-state under communism? Why?

Edmund Burke, Reflections on the Revolution in France
(1790)

Born and raised in Ireland, Burke became a member of Britain's Parliament, an accomplished orator, and influential political philosopher. Though supportive of the American Revolution of 1776, as can be seen here, he viewed its sister, the French Revolution of 1789, quite differently. He is best known today as an architect of modern conservative thought.

You [*in France—Ed.*] might, if you pleased, have profited of our example, and have given to your recovered freedom a correspondent dignity. Your privileges, though discontinued, were not lost to memory. Your constitution, it is true, whilst you were out of possession, suffered waste and dilapidation; but you possessed in some parts the walls, and, in all, the foundations, of a noble and venerable castle. You might have repaired those walls; you might have built on those old foundations. Your constitution was suspended before it was perfected; but you had the elements of a constitution very nearly as good as could be wished. . . .

You had all these advantages in your ancient states; but you chose to act as if you had never been moulded into civil society, and had everything to begin anew. You began ill, because you began by despising everything that belonged to you. You set up your trade without a capital. If the last generations of your country appeared without much lustre in you eyes, you might have passed them by, and derived your claims from a more early race of ancestors. Under a pious predilection for those ancestors, your imaginations would have realized in them a standard of virtue and wisdom, beyond the vulgar practice of the hour; and you would have risen with the example to whose imitation you aspired. Respecting your forefathers, you would have been taught to respect yourselves. You would not have chosen to consider the French as a people of yesterday, as a nation of low-born servile wretches until the emancipating year of 1789. . . .

By following wise examples you would have given new examples of wisdom to the world. You would have rendered the cause of liberty venerable in the eyes of every worthy mind in every nation. You would have shamed despotism from the earth, by showing that freedom was not only reconcilable, but, as when well disciplined it is, auxiliary to law. You would have had an unoppressive but a productive revenue. You would have had a flourishing commerce to feed it. You would have had a free constitution; a potent monarchy; a disciplined army; a reformed and venerated clergy; mitigated but spirited nobility, to lead your virtue, not to overlay it; you would have had a liberal order of commons, to emulate and to recruit that nobility; you would have had a protected, satisfied, laborious, and obedient people, taught to seek and to recognise the happiness that is to be found by virtue in all conditions; in which

---

From *Reflections on the French Revolution* by Edmund Burke, The Harvard Classics, 1909–1914.

consists the true moral equality of mankind, and not in that monstrous fiction, which, by inspiring false ideas and vain expectations into men destined to travel in the obscure walk of laborious life, serves only to aggravate and embitter that real inequality, which it never can remove; and which the order of civil life establishes as much for the benefit of those whom it must leave in an humble state, as those whom it is able to exalt to a condition more splendid, but not more happy. You had a smooth and easy career of felicity and glory laid open to you, beyond anything recorded in the history of the world; but you have shown that difficulty is good for man.

Compute your gains: see what is got by those extravagant and presumptuous speculations which have taught your leaders to despise all their predecessors, and all their contemporaries, and even to despise themselves, until the moment in which they became truly despicable. By following those false lights, France has bought undisguised calamities at a higher price than any nation has purchased the most unequivocal blessings! France has bought poverty by crime! France has not sacrificed her virtue to her interest, but she has abandoned her interest, that she might prostitute her virtue. All other nations have begun the fabric of a new government, or the reformation of an old, by establishing originally, or by enforcing with greater exactness, some rites or other of religion. All other people have laid the foundations of civil freedom in severer manners, and a system of a more austere and masculine morality. France, when she let loose the reins of regal authority, doubled the license of a ferocious dissoluteness in manners, and of an insolent irreligion in opinions and practices; and has extended through all ranks of life, as if she were communicating some privilege, or laying open some secluded benefit, all the unhappy corruptions that usually were the disease of wealth and power. This is one of the new principles of equality in France.

This was unnatural. The rest is in order. They have found their punishment in their success. Laws overturned; tribunals subverted; industry without vigour; commerce expiring; the revenue unpaid, yet the people impoverished; a church pillaged, and a state not relieved; civil and military anarchy made the constitution of the kingdom; everything human and divine sacrificed to the idol of public credit, and national bankruptcy the consequence....

Were all these dreadful things necessary? Were they the inevitable results of the desperate struggle of determined patriots, compelled to wade through blood and tumult to the quiet shore of a tranquil and prosperous liberty? No! Nothing like it. The fresh ruins of France, which shock our feelings wherever we can turn our eyes, are not devastation of civil war; they are the sad but instructive monuments of rash and ignorant counsel in time of profound peace....

The science of government being therefore so practical in itself, and intended for such practical purposes, a matter which requires experience, and even more experience than any person can gain in his whole life, however sagacious and observing he may be, it is with infinite caution that any man ought to venture upon pulling down an edifice, which has answered in any tolerable degree for ages the common purposes of society, or on building it up again, without having models and patterns of approved utility before his eyes....

When ancient opinions and rules of life are taken away, the loss cannot possibly be estimated. From that moment we have no compass to govern us; nor can we know distinctly to what port we steer. Europe, undoubtedly, taken in a mass, was in a flourishing condition the day on which your revolution was completed. How much of that prosperous state was owing to the spirit of our old manners and opinions is not easy to say; but as such causes cannot be indifferent in their operation, we must presume, that, on the whole, their operation was beneficial....

Four hundred years have gone over us; but I believe we are not materially changed since that period. Thanks to our sullen resistance to innovation, thanks to the cold sluggishness of our national character, we still bear the stamp of our forefathers. We have not (as I conceive) lost the generosity and dignity of thinking of the fourteenth century; nor as yet have we subtilized ourselves into savages. We are not the converts of Rousseau; we are not the disciples of Voltaire; Helvetius has made no progress amongst us.[1] Atheists are not our preachers; madmen are not our lawgivers. We know that *we*

---

[1] Burke refers to Rousseau, Voltaire, and Helvetius because they were 18th century Enlightenment philosophers whose ideas were considered radical by conservatives of this time period. Rousseau's ideas, particularly the concept of the "general will", influenced and inspired the French Revolution; Voltaire promoted the rights of man and defended civil liberties, such as freedom of religion and freedom of the press; and Helvetius argued that all people are born intellectually equal and that all human behavior is determined by education and environment.

have made no discoveries, and we think that no discoveries are to be made, in morality; nor many in the great principles of government, nor in the ideas of liberty, which were understood long before we were born, altogether as well as they will be after the grave has heaped its mould upon our presumption, and the silent tomb shall have imposed its law on our pert loquacity.... We fear God; we look up with awe to kings; with affection to parliaments; with duty to magistrates; with reverence to priests; and with respect to nobility....

We are afraid to put men to live and trade each on his own private stock of reason; because we suspect that this stock in each man is small, and that the individuals would do better to avail themselves of the general bank and capital of nations and of ages. Many of our men of speculation, instead of exploding general prejudices, employ their sagacity to discover the latent wisdom which prevails in them.

Critical Thinking Questions

1. What has been the result of the French Revolution, according to Burke? Why has it failed?

2. What is Burke's view of social equality?

3. What does Burke appear to think of the average individual?

4. In your opinion, which paragraph best highlights or summarizes Burke's general conservative philosophy? Justify your answer.

John Stuart Mill, "On Liberty"
(1859)

John Stuart Mill was a British economist and philosopher. His celebrated essay, "On Liberty," which is excerpted here, remains to this day one of the most influential statements of liberal thought. It is concerned primarily with defining the appropriate limits that should be placed on the authority of governments and laws over individuals.

The object of this Essay is to assert one very simple principle, as entitled to govern absolutely the dealings of society with the individual in the way of compulsion and control, whether the means used be physical force in the form of legal penalties, or the moral coercion of public opinion. That principle is, that the sole end for which mankind are warranted, individually or collectively, in interfering with the liberty of action of any of their number, is self-protection. That the only purpose for which power can be rightfully exercised over any member of a civilized community, against his will, is to prevent harm to others. His own good, either physical or moral, is not a sufficient warrant.

. . .

. . . The only freedom which deserves the name, is that of pursuing our own good in our own way, so long as we do not attempt to deprive others of theirs, or impede their efforts to obtain it. Each is the proper guardian of his own health, whether bodily, or mental and spiritual. Mankind are greater gainers by suffering each other to live as seems good to themselves, than by compelling each to live as seems good to the rest.

. . .

We have now recognised the necessity to the mental well-being of mankind (on which all their other well-being depends) of freedom of opinion, and freedom of the expression of opinion, on four distinct grounds; which we will now briefly recapitulate.

First, if any opinion is compelled to silence, that opinion may, for aught we can certainly know, be true. To deny this is to assume our own infallibility.

Secondly, though the silenced opinion be an error, it may, and very commonly does, contain a portion of truth; and since the general or prevailing opinion on any subject is rarely or never the whole truth, it is only by the collision of adverse opinions that the remainder of the truth has any chance of being supplied.

Thirdly, even if the received opinion be not only true, but the whole truth; unless it is suffered to be, and actually is, vigorously and earnestly contested, it will, by most of those who receive it, be held in the manner of a prejudice, with little comprehension or feeling of its rational grounds. And not only this, but, fourthly, the meaning of the doctrine itself will be in danger of being lost, or enfeebled, and deprived of its vital effect on the character and conduct: the dogma becoming a mere formal profession, inefficacious for good, but cumbering the ground, and preventing the growth of any real and heartfelt conviction, from reason or personal experience.

Before quitting the subject of freedom of opinion, it is fit to take some notice of those who say, that the free expression of all opinions should be

---

From *On Liberty*, by John Stuart Mill, 1859.

permitted, on condition that the manner be temperate, and do not pass the bounds of fair discussion. Much might be said on the impossibility of fixing where these supposed bounds are to be placed; for if the test be offence to those whose opinion is attacked, I think experience testifies that this offence is given whenever the attack is telling and powerful, and that every opponent who pushes them hard, and whom they find it difficult to answer, appears to them, if he shows any strong feeling on the subject, an intemperate opponent. But this, though an important consideration in a practical point of view, merges in a more fundamental objection. Undoubtedly the manner of asserting an opinion, even though it be a true one, may be very objectionable, and may justly incur severe censure. But the principal offences of the kind are such as it is mostly impossible, unless by accidental self-betrayal, to bring home to conviction. The gravest of them is, to argue sophistically, to suppress facts or arguments, to misstate the elements of the case, or misrepresent the opposite opinion. But all this, even to the most aggravated degree, is so continually done in perfect good faith, by persons who are not considered, and in many other respects may not deserve to be considered, ignorant or incompetent, that it is rarely possible on adequate grounds conscientiously to stamp the misrepresentation as morally culpable; and still less could law presume to interfere with this kind of controversial misconduct. With regard to what is commonly meant by intemperate discussion, namely invective, sarcasm, personality, and the like, the denunciation of these weapons would deserve more sympathy if it were ever proposed to interdict them equally to both sides; but it is only desired to restrain the employment of them against the prevailing opinion: against the unprevailing they may not only be used without general disapproval, but will be likely to obtain for him who uses them the praise of honest zeal and righteous indignation. Yet whatever mischief arises from their use, is greatest when they are employed against the comparatively defenceless; and whatever unfair advantage can be derived by any opinion from this mode of asserting it, accrues almost exclusively to received opinions. The worst offence of this kind which can be committed by a polemic, is to stigmatize those who hold the contrary opinion as bad and immoral men. To calumny of this sort, those who hold any unpopular opinion are peculiarly exposed, because they are in general few and uninfluential, and nobody but themselves feels much interested in seeing justice done them; but this weapon is, from the nature of the case, denied to those who attack a prevailing opinion: they can neither use it with safety to themselves, nor, if they could, would it do anything but recoil on their own cause. In general, opinions contrary to those commonly received can only obtain a hearing by studied moderation of language, and the most cautious avoidance of unnecessary offence, from which they hardly ever deviate even in a slight degree without losing ground: while unmeasured vituperation employed on the side of the prevailing opinion, really does deter people from professing contrary opinions, and from listening to those who profess them. For the interest, therefore, of truth and justice, it is far more important to restrain this employment of vituperative language than the other; and, for example, if it were necessary to choose, there would be much more need to discourage offensive attacks on infidelity, than on religion. It is, however, obvious that law and authority have no business with restraining either, while opinion ought, in every instance, to determine its verdict by the circumstances of the individual case; condemning every one, on whichever side of the argument he places himself, in whose mode of advocacy either want of candour, or malignity, bigotry, or intolerance of feeling manifest themselves; but not inferring these vices from the side which a person takes, though it be the contrary side of the question to our own: and giving merited honour to every one, whatever opinion he may hold, who has calmness to see and honesty to state what his opponents and their opinions really are, exaggerating nothing to their discredit, keeping nothing back which tells, or can be supposed to tell, in their favour. This is the real morality of public discussion: and if often violated, I am happy to think that there are many controversialists who to a great extent observe it, and a still greater number who consciously strive towards it.

Critical Thinking Questions

1. According to Mill, when is society justified in restricting liberty?

2. Why is freedom of opinion and expression necessary in society? On what grounds is it necessary?

3. In your opinion, which single sentence best encapsulates or reflects the overall drift of the document? Justify your answer.

Giuseppe Mazzini on Nationalism
(1852)

Mazzini was a leading proponent of Italian unification. The following is extracted from his 1852 essay, "Europe: Its Conditions and Prospects."

Europe no longer possesses unity of faith, of mission, or of aim. Such unity is a necessity in the world. Here, then, is the secret of the crisis. It is the duty of every one to examine and analyse calmly and carefully the probable elements of this new unity. But those who persist in perpetuating, by violence or by Jesuitical compromise, the external observance of the old unity, only perpetuate the crisis, and render its issue more violent.

. . .

There are in Europe two great questions; or, rather, the question of the transformation of authority, that is to say, of the Revolution, has assumed two forms; the question which all have agreed to call social, and the question of nationalities. The first is more exclusively agitated in France, the second in the heart of the other peoples of Europe. I say, *which all have agreed to call social,* because, generally speaking, every great revolution is so far social, that it cannot be accomplished either in the religious, political, or any other sphere, without affecting social relations, the sources and the distribution of wealth; but that which is only a secondary consequence in political revolutions is now the cause and the banner of the movement in France. The question there is now, above all, to establish better relations between labour and capital, between production and consumption, between the workman and the employer.

It is probable that the European initiative, that which will give a new impulse to intelligence and to events, will spring from the question of nationalities. The social question may, in effect, although with difficulty, be partly resolved by a single people; it is an internal question for each, and the French Republicans of 1848 so understood it, when, determinately abandoning the European initiative, they placed Lamartine's manifesto by the side of their aspirations towards the organisation of labour. The question of nationality can only be resolved by destroying the treaties of 1815, and changing the map of Europe and its public Law. The question of *Nationalities,* rightly understood, is the Alliance of the Peoples; the balance of powers based upon new foundations; the organisation of the work that Europe has to accomplish.

. . .

It was not for a material interest that the people of Vienna fought in 1848; in weakening the empire they could only lose power. It was not for an increase of wealth that the people of Lombardy fought in the same year; the Austrian Government had endeavoured in the year preceding to excite the peasants against the landed proprietors, as they had done in Gallicia; but everywhere they had failed. They struggled, they still struggle, as do Poland, Germany, and Hungary, for country and liberty; for a word inscribed upon a banner, proclaiming to the world

---

From *Writings, Literary, Political and Religious* of Joseph Mazzini, London: Walter Scott, 1880.

that they also live, think, love, and labour for the benefit of all. They speak the same language, they bear about them the impress of consanguinity, they kneel beside the same tombs, they glory in the same tradition; and they demand to associate freely, without obstacles, without foreign domination, in order to elaborate and express their idea; to contribute their stone also to the great pyramid of history. It is something moral which they are seeking; and this moral something is in fact, even politically speaking, the most important question in the present state of things. It is the organisation of the European task. It is no longer the savage, hostile, quarrelsome nationality of two hundred years ago which is invoked by these peoples. The nationality . . . founded upon the following principle:—*Whichever people, by its superiority of strength, and by its geographical position, can do us an injury, is our natural enemy; whichever cannot do us an injury, but can by the amount of its force and by its position injure our enemy, is our natural ally,*—is the princely nationality of aristocracies or royal races. The nationality of the peoples has not these dangers; it can only be founded by a common effort and a common movement; sympathy and alliance will be its result. In principle, as in the ideas formerly laid down by the men influencing every national party, nationality ought only to be to humanity that which the division of labour is in a workshop—the recognised symbol of association; the assertion of the individuality of a human group called by its geographical position, its traditions, and its language, to fulfil a special function in the European work of civilisation.

The map of Europe has to be re-made. This is the key to the present movement; herein lies the initiative. Before acting, the instrument for action must be organised; before building, the ground must be one's own. The social idea cannot be realised under any form whatsoever before this reorganisation of Europe is effected; before the peoples are free to interrogate themselves; to express their vocation, and to assure its accomplishment by an alliance capable of substituting itself for the absolutist league which now reigns supreme.

Critical Thinking Questions

1. According to Mazzini, what is a nation? What are its identifying characteristics?

2. What did Mazzini think was wrong with the existing system of European states?

3. What changes needed to be made in Europe in order to make nationalist movements successful?

Simón de Bolívar Addresses the Congress of Angostura
(1819)

Bolívar was born in Venezuela and lived from 1783 to 1830. Popularly known as "El Liberator," he was instrumental in ending Spanish control over large areas of South America. In 1819 Bolívar became the first president of Colombia (which then included also the current states of Ecuador, Panama, and Venezuela). In a speech to the Congress of Angostura (now Ciudad Bolívar in Venezuela), he offered a definition of Latin American national identity.

We are not Europeans; we are not Indians; we are but a mixed species of aborigines and Spaniards. Americans by birth and Europeans by law, we find ourselves engaged in a dual conflict: we are disputing with the natives for titles of ownership, and at the same time we are struggling to maintain ourselves in the country that gave us birth against the opposition of the invaders. Thus our position is most extraordinary and complicated. But there is more. As our role has always been strictly passive and political existence nil, we find that our quest for liberty is now even more difficult of accomplishment; for we, having been placed in a state lower than slavery, had been robbed not only of our freedom but also of the right to exercise an active domestic tyranny . . . We have been ruled more by deceit than by force, and we have been degraded more by vice than by superstition. Slavery is the daughter of darkness: an ignorant people is a blind instrument of its own destruction. Ambition and intrigue abuses the credulity and experience of men lacking all political, economic, and civic knowledge; they adopt pure illusion as reality; they take license for liberty, treachery for patriotism, and vengeance for justice. If a people, perverted by their training, succeed in achieving their liberty, they will soon lose it, for it would be of no avail to endeavor to explain to them that happiness consists in the practice of virtue; that the rule of law is more powerful than the rule of tyrants, because, as the laws are more inflexible, every one should submit to their beneficent austerity; that proper morals, and not force, are the bases of law; and that to practice justice is to practice liberty.

Although those people [North Americans], so lacking in many respects, are unique in the history of mankind, it is a marvel, I repeat, that so weak and complicated a government as the federal system has managed to govern them in the difficult and trying circumstances of their past. But, regardless of the effectiveness of this form of government with respect to North America, I must say that it has never for a moment entered my mind to compare the position and character of two states as dissimilar as the English-American and the Spanish-American. Would it not be most difficult to apply to Spain and English system of political, civil, and religious liberty: Hence, it would be even more difficult to adapt to Venezuela the laws of North America.

From Simon DeBolivar, An Address to Bolivar at the Congress of Angostura, 1819.

Nothing in our fundamental laws would have to be altered were we to adopt a legislative power similar to that held by the British Parliament. Like the North Americans, we have divided national representation into two chambers: that of Representatives and the Senate. The first is very wisely constituted. It enjoys all its proper functions, and it requires no essential revision, because the Constitution, in creating it, gave it the form and powers which the people deemed necessary in order that they might be legally and properly represented. If the Senate were hereditary rather than elective, it would, in my opinion, be the basis, the tie, the very soul of our republic. In political storms this body would arrest the thunderbolts of the government and would repel any violent popular reaction. Devoted to the government because of a natural interest in its own preservation, a hereditary senate would always oppose any attempt on the part of the people to infringe upon the jurisdiction and authority of their magistrates . . . The creation of a hereditary senate would in no way be a violation of political equality. I do not solicit the establishment of a nobility, for as a celebrated republican has said, that would simultaneously destroy equality and liberty. What I propose is an office for which the candidates must prepare themselves, an office that demands great knowledge and the ability to acquire such knowledge. All should not be left to chance and the outcome of elections. The people are more easily deceived than is Nature perfected by art; and although these senators, it is true, would not be bred in an environment that is all virtue, it is equally true that they would be raised in an atmosphere of enlightened education. The hereditary senate will also serve as a counterweight to both government and people; and as a neutral power it will weaken the mutual attacks of these two eternally rival powers.

The British executive power possesses all the authority properly appertaining to a sovereign, but he is surrounded by a triple line of dams, barriers, and stockades. He is the head of government, but his ministers and subordinates rely more upon law than upon his authority, as they are personally responsible; and not even decrees of royal authority can exempt them from this responsibility. The executive is commander in chief of the army and navy; he makes peace and declares war; but Parliament annually determines what sums are to be paid to these military forces. While the courts and judges are dependent on the executive power, the laws originate in and are made by Parliament. Give Venezuela such as executive power in the person of a president chosen by the people or their representatives, and you will have taken a great step toward national happiness. No matter what citizen occupies this office, he will be aided by the Constitution, and therein being authorized to do good, he can do no harm, because his ministers will cooperate with him only insofar as he abides by the law. If he attempts to infringe upon the law, his own ministers will desert him, thereby isolating him from the Republic, and they will even bring charges against him in the Senate. The ministers, being responsible for any transgressions committed, will actually govern, since they must account for their actions.

A republican magistrate is an individual set apart from society, charged with checking the impulse of the people toward license and the propensity of judges and administrators toward abuse of the laws. He is directly subject to the legislative body, the senate, and the people: he is the one man who resists the combined pressure of the opinions, interests, and passions of the social state and who, as Carnot states, does little more than struggle constantly with the urge to dominate and the desire to escape domination. This weakness can only be corrected by a strongly rooted force. It should be strongly proportioned to meet the resistance which the executive must expect from the legislature, from the judiciary, and from the people of a republic. Unless the executive has easy access to all the administrative resources, fixed by a just distribution of powers, he inevitably becomes a nonentity or abuses his authority. By this I mean that the result will be the death of the government, whose heirs are anarchy, usurpation, and tyranny . . . Therefore, let the entire system of government be strengthened, and let the balance of power be drawn up in such a manner that it will be permanent and incapable of decay because of its own tenuity. Precisely because no form of government is so weak as the democratic, its framework must be firmer, and its institutions must be studied to determine their degree of stability . . . unless this is done, we will have to reckon with an ungovernable, tumultuous, and anarchic society, not with a social order where happiness, peace, and justice prevail.

Critical Thinking Questions

1. According to Bolívar, what are the distinguishing characteristics of Latin Americans?

2. What features or characteristics does Bolívar believe the government of his country should have? Specifically, what type of legislative and executive institutions should Venezuela have?

Theodor Herzl and Zionism
(1896)

Theodor Herzl was a Jewish journalist born and raised in what is today Hungary. His pamphlet, The Jewish State, *which was published in 1896, became the founding document of a Jewish nationalism known as Zionism (after the biblical name for the Promised Land).*

The idea which I have developed in this pamphlet is a very old one: it is the restoration of the Jewish State.

The world resounds with outcries against the Jews, and these outcries have awakened the slumbering idea.

. . .

We are a people—one people.

We have honestly endeavored everywhere to merge ourselves in the social life of surrounding communities and to preserve the faith of our fathers. We are not permitted to do so. In vain are we loyal patriots, our loyalty in some places running to extremes; in vain do we make the same sacrifices of life and property as our fellow citizens; in vain do we strive to increase the fame of our native land in science and art, or her wealth by trade and commerce. In countries where we have lived for centuries we are still cried down as strangers, and often by those whose ancestors were not yet domiciled in the land where Jews had already had experience of suffering. The majority may decide which are the strangers; for this, as indeed every point which arises in the relations between nations, is a question of might. I do not here surrender any portion of our prescriptive right, when I make this statement merely in my own name as an individual. In the world as it now is and for an indefinite period will probably remain, might precedes right. It is useless, therefore, for us to be loyal patriots, as were the Huguenots who were forced to emigrate. If we could only be left in peace. . . .

. . .

[However,] oppression and persecution cannot exterminate us. No nation on earth has survived such struggles and sufferings as we have gone through. Jew-baiting has merely stripped off our weaklings; the strong among us were invariably true to their race when persecution broke out against them. . . .

However much I may worship personality—powerful individual personality in statesmen, inventors, artists, philosophers, or leaders, as well as the collective personality of a historic group of human beings, which we call a nation—however much I may worship personality, I do not regret its disappearance. Whoever can, will, and must perish, let him perish. But the distinctive nationality of Jews neither can, will, nor must be destroyed. It cannot be destroyed, because external enemies consolidate it. It will not be destroyed; this is shown during two thousand years of appalling suffering. It must not be destroyed . . . Whole branches of Judaism may wither and fall, but the trunk will remain.

From *The Jewish State: An Attempt at a Modern Solution to the Jewish Question*, American Zionist Emergency Council, 1946. Reprinted with permission.

The Jewish Question

No one can deny the gravity of the situation of the Jews. Wherever they live in perceptible numbers, they are more or less persecuted. Their equality before the law, granted by statute, has become practically a dead letter. They are debarred from filling even moderately high positions, either in the army, or in any public or private capacity. And attempts are made to thrust them out of business also: "Don't buy from Jews!"

Attacks in Parliaments, in assemblies, in the press, in the pulpit, in the street, on journeys—for example, their exclusion from certain hotels—even in places of recreation, become daily more numerous. The forms of persecutions varying according to the countries and social circles in which they occur....

The Plan

Let the sovereignty be granted us over a portion of the globe large enough to satisfy the rightful requirements of a nation; the rest we shall manage for ourselves.

The creation of a new State is neither ridiculous nor impossible. We have in our day witnessed the process in connection with nations which were not largely members of the middle class, but poorer, less educated, and consequently weaker than ourselves. The Governments of all countries scourged by Anti-Semitism will be keenly interested in assisting us to obtain the sovereignty we want.

The plan, simple in design, but complicated in execution, will be carried out by two agencies: The Society of Jews and the Jewish Company.

The Society of Jews will do the preparatory work in the domains of science and politics, which the Jewish Company will afterwards apply practically.

The Jewish Company will be the liquidating agent of the business interests of departing Jews, and will organize commerce and trade in the new country.

We must not imagine the departure of the Jews to be a sudden one. It will be gradual, continuous, and will cover many decades. The poorest will go first to cultivate the soil. In accordance with a preconceived plan, they will construct roads, bridges, railways and telegraph installations; regulate rivers; and build their own dwellings; their labor will create trade, trade will create markets and markets will attract new settlers, for every man will go voluntarily, at his own expense and his own risk. The labor expended on the land will enhance its value, and the Jews will soon perceive that a new and permanent sphere of operation is opening here for that spirit of enterprise which has heretofore met only with hatred and obloquy.

Critical Thinking Questions

1. According to Herzl, why do the Jews need a state of their own?

2. What do you think Herzl may be referring to in saying (in paragraph 5) that "Jew-baiting has merely stripped off our weaklings; the strong among us were invariably true to their race when persecution broke out against them?"

3. Herzl advocated for the restoration of a Jewish state in Palestine, laying the basis for modern day Israel. Generally speaking, why might the choice of this location be a source of conflict for the future?

Charles Darwin, The Descent of Man
(1871)

Darwin's most famous book was, and remains, The Origins of the Species, *first published in 1859. The book introduced the theory of evolution by means of natural selection but focused almost entirely on plants and animals. Darwin's contention that human beings were also the products of the same long process of evolution came in a later book entitled* The Descent of Man, *from which the following is taken.*

The main conclusion here arrived at, and now held by many naturalists who are well competent to form a sound judgment, is that man is descended from some less highly organised form. The grounds upon which this conclusion rests will never be shaken, for the close similarity between man and the lower animals in embryonic development, as well as in innumerable points of structure and constitution, both of high and of the most trifling importance,—the rudiments which he retains, and the abnormal revisions to which he is occasionally liable,—are facts which cannot be disputed. They have long been known, but until recently they told us nothing with respect to the origin of man. Now when viewed by the light of our knowledge of the whole organic world their meaning is unmistakable. The great principle of evolution stands up clear and firm, when these groups of facts are considered in connection with others, such as the mutual affinities of the members of the same group, their geographical distribution in past and present times, and their geological succession. It is incredible that all these facts should speak falsely. He who is not content to look, like a savage, at the phenomena of nature as disconnected, cannot any longer believe that man is the work of a separate act of creation. He will be forced to admit that the close resemblance of the embryo of man to that, for instance, of a dog—the construction of his skull, limbs and whole frame on the same plan with that of other mammals, independently of the uses to which the parts may be put—the occasional reappearance of various structures, for instance of several muscles, which man does not normally possess, but which are common to the Quadrumana—and a crowd of analogous facts—all point in the plainest manner to the conclusion that man is the co-descendant with other mammals of a common progenitor.

We have seen that man incessantly presents individual differences in all parts of his body and in his mental faculties. These differences or variations seem to be induced by the same general causes, and to obey the same laws as with the lower animals. In both cases similar laws of inheritance prevail. Man tends to increase at a greater rate than his means of subsistence; consequently he is occasionally subjected to a severe struggle for existence, and natural selection will have effected whatever lies within its scope. A succession of strongly-marked variations of a similar nature is by no means requisite; slight fluctuating differences in the individual suffice for the work of natural selection; not that we have any reason to suppose that in the same species, all parts of the organisation tend to vary to the same degree.

From *The Descent of Man* and selections in relation to Sex, 1883.

By considering the embryological structure of man,—the homologies which he presents with the lower animals,—the rudiments which he retains,—and the reversions to which he is liable, we can partly recall in imagination the former condition of our early progenitors; and can approximately place them in their proper place in the zoological series. We thus learn that man is descended from a hairy, tailed quadruped, probably arboreal in its habits, and an inhabitant of the Old World. This creature, if its whole structure had been examined by a naturalist, would have been classed amongst the Quadrumana, as surely as the still more ancient progenitor of the Old and New World monkeys. The Quadrumana and all the higher mammals are probably derived from an ancient marsupial animal, and this through a long line of diversified forms, from some amphibian-like creature, and this again from some fish-like animal. In the dim obscurity of the past we can see that the early progenitor of all the Vertebrata must have been an aquatic animal, provided with branchiæ, with the two sexes united in the same individual, and with the most important organs of the body (such as the brain and heart) imperfectly or not at all developed. This animal seems to have been more like the larvæ of the existing marine Ascidians than any other known form.

The high standard of our intellectual powers and moral disposition is the greatest difficulty which presents itself, after we have been driven to this conclusion on the origin of man. But every one who admits the principle of evolution, must see that the mental powers of the higher animals, which are the same in kind with those of man, though so different in degree, are capable of advancement....

The moral nature of man has reached its present standard, partly through the advancement of his reasoning powers and consequently of a just public opinion, but especially from his sympathies having been rendered more tender and widely diffused through the effects of habit, example, instruction, and reflection. It is not improbable that after long practice virtuous tendencies may be inherited. With the more civilised races, the conviction of the existence of an all-seeing Deity has had a potent influence on the advance of morality. Ultimately man does not accept the praise or blame of his fellows as his sole guide though few escape this influence, but his habitual convictions, controlled by reason, afford him the safest rule. His conscience then becomes the supreme judge and monitor. Nevertheless the first foundation or origin of the moral sense lies in the social instincts, including sympathy; and these instincts no doubt were primarily gained, as in the case of the lower animals, through natural selection.

The belief in God has often been advanced as not only the greatest but the most complete of all the distinctions between man and the lower animals. It is however impossible, as we have seen, to maintain that this belief is innate or instinctive in man. On the other hand a belief in all-pervading spiritual agencies seems to be universal, and apparently follows from a considerable advance in man's reason, and from a still greater advance in his faculties of imagination, curiosity and wonder. I am aware that the assumed instinctive belief in God has been used by many persons as an argument for His existence. But this is a rash argument, as we should thus be compelled to believe in the existence of many cruel and malignant spirits, only a little more powerful than man; for the belief in them is far more general than in a beneficent Deity. The idea of a universal and beneficent Creator does not seem to arise in the mind of man, until he has been elevated by long-continued culture....

I am aware that the conclusions arrived at in this work will be denounced by some as highly irreligious; but he who denounces them is bound to shew why it is more irreligious to explain the origin of man as a distinct species by descent from some lower form, through the laws of variation and natural selection, than to explain the birth of the individual through the laws of ordinary reproduction. The birth both of the species and of the individual are equally parts of that grand sequence of events, which our minds refuse to accept as the result of blind chance. The understanding revolts at such a conclusion, whether or not we are able to believe that every slight variation of structure,—the union of each pair in marriage,—the dissemination of each seed,—and other such events, have all been ordained for some special purpose.

Sexual selection has been treated at great length in this work, for, as I have attempted to shew, it has played an important part in the history of the organic world. I am aware that much remains doubtful, but I have endeavoured to give a fair view of the whole case. In the lower divisions of the animal kingdom, sexual selection seems to have done nothing: such animals are often affixed for life to the same spot, or have the sexes combined in the same individual, or what is still more important, their perceptive and intellectual faculties are not sufficiently advanced to allow of the feelings of love and jealousy, or of the exertion of choice. When, however, we come to the Arthropoda and Vertebrata, even to the lowest classes in these two great—Sub-Kingdoms, sexual selection has effected much....

Sexual selection depends on the success of certain individuals over others of the same sex, in relation to the propagation of the species; whilst natural selection depends on the success of both sexes, at all ages, in relation to the general conditions of life. The sexual struggle is of two kinds; in the one it is between the individuals of the same sex, generally the males, in order to drive away or kill their rivals, the females remaining passive; whilst in the other, the struggle is likewise between the individuals of the same sex, in order to excite or charm those of the opposite sex, generally the females, which no longer remain passive, but select the more agreeable partners....

The main conclusion arrived at in this work, namely that man is descended from some lowly organised form, will, I regret to think, be highly distasteful to many. But there can hardly be a doubt that we are descended from barbarians. The astonishment which I felt on first seeing a party of Fuegians on a wild and broken shore will never be forgotten by me,—for the reflection at once rushed into my mind—such were our ancestors. These men were absolutely naked and bedaubed with paint, their long hair was tangled, their mouths frothed with excitement, and their expression was wild, startled, and distrustful. They possessed hardly any arts, and like wild animals lived on what they could catch; they had no government, and were merciless to every one not of their own small tribe. He who has seen a savage in his native land will not feel much shame, if forced to acknowledge that the blood of some more humble creature flows in his veins. For my own part I would as soon be descended from that heroic little monkey, who braved his dreaded enemy in order to save the life of his keeper, or from that old baboon, who descending from the mountains, carried away in triumph his young comrade from a crowd of astonished dogs—as from a savage who delights to torture his enemies, offers up bloody sacrifices, practises infanticide without remorse, treats his wives like slaves, knows no decency, and is haunted by the grossest superstitions.

Man may be excused for feeling some pride at having risen, though not through his own exertions, to the very summit of the organic scale; and the fact of his having thus risen, instead of having been aboriginally placed there, may give him hope for a still higher destiny in the distant future. But we are not here concerned with hopes or fears, only with the truth as far as our reason permits us to discover it; and I have given the evidence to the best of my ability. We must, however, acknowledge, as it seems to me, that man with all his noble qualities, with sympathy which feels for the most debased, with benevolence which extends not only to other men but to the humblest living creature, with his god-like intellect which has penetrated into the movements and constitution of the solar system—with all these exalted powers—Man still bears in his bodily frame the indelible stamp of his lowly origin.

Critical Thinking Questions

1. What do you think Darwin considers to be his best evidence in favor of human beings having evolved through natural selection?

2. What does Darwin appear to think about belief in God?

3. Darwin focuses mostly on humanity's evolutionary *past*. What does he say about our possible future, though? And what evidence does he give for his "predictions?"

The New Imperialism

Jules Ferry Discusses French Colonialism (1884)

Europeans Carve Up the African "Cake" at Berlin (1885)

Rudyard Kipling, The White Man's Burden *(1899)*

Jules Ferry Discusses French Colonialism
(1884)

Jules Ferry was French prime minister during much of the first half of the 1880s. Here he outlines the purposes and prospects of French colonial expansion.

The policy of colonial expansion is a political and economic system . . . that can be connected to three sets of ideas: economic ideas; the most far-reaching ideas of civilization; and ideas of a political and patriotic sort.

In the area of economics, I am placing before you, with the support of some statistics, the considerations that justify the policy of colonial expansion, as seen from the perspective of a need, felt more and more urgently by the industrialized population of Europe and especially the people of our rich and hardworking country of France: the need for outlets [for exports]. Is this a fantasy? Is this a concern [that can wait] for the future? Or is this not a pressing need, one may say a crying need, of our industrial population? I merely express in a general way what each one of you can see for himself in the various parts of France. Yes, what our major industries, irrevocably steered by the treaties of 1860 into exports, lack more and more are outlets. Why? Because next door Germany is setting up trade barriers; because across the ocean the United States of America have become protectionists, and extreme protectionists at that; because not only are these great markets . . . shrinking, becoming more and more difficult of access, but these great states are beginning to pour into our own markets products not seen there before. This is true not only for our agriculture, which has been so sorely tried . . . and for which competition is no longer limited to the circle of large European states. . . . Today, as you know, competition, the law of supply and demand, freedom of trade, the effects of speculation, all radiate in a circle that reaches to the ends of the earth. . . . That is a great complication, a great economic difficulty; . . . an extremely serious problem. It is so serious, gentlemen, so acute, that the least informed persons must already glimpse, foresee, and take precautions against the time when the great South American market that has, in a manner of speaking, belonged to us forever will be disputed and perhaps taken away from us by North American products. Nothing is more serious; there can be no graver social problem; and these matters are linked intimately to colonial policy.

Gentlemen, we must speak more loudly and more honestly! We must say openly that indeed the higher races have a right over the lower races. . . .

I repeat, that the superior races have a right because they have a duty. They have the duty to civilize the inferior races. . . . In the history of earlier centuries these duties, gentlemen, have often been misunderstood; and certainly when the Spanish soldiers and explorers introduced slavery into Central America, they did not fulfill their duty as men of a higher race. . . . But, in our time, I maintain that European nations acquit themselves with generosity, with grandeur, and with sincerity of this superior civilizing duty.

From Jules Francois Camille Ferry "Speech Before the French Chamber of Deputies, March 28, 1884, translated by Ruth Kleinman, Brooklyn College Core Four Sourcebook.

I say that French colonial policy, the policy of colonial expansion, the policy that has taken us under the Empire to Saigon, to Indochina [Vietnam], that has led us to Tunisia, to Madagascar—I say that this policy of colonial expansion was inspired by . . . the fact that a navy such as ours cannot do without safe harbors, defenses, supply centers on the high seas. . . . Are you unaware of this? Look at a map of the world.

Gentlemen, these are considerations that merit the full attention of patriots. The conditions of naval warfare have greatly changed. . . . At present, as you know, a warship, however perfect its design, cannot carry more than two weeks' supply of coal; and a vessel without coal is a wreck on the high seas, abandoned to the first occupier. Hence the need to have places of supply, shelters, ports for defense and provisioning. . . . And that is why we needed Tunisia; that is why we needed Saigon and Indochina; that is why we need Madagascar . . . and why we shall never leave them! . . . Gentlemen, in Europe such as it is today, in this competition of the many rivals we see rising up around us, some by military or naval improvements, others by the prodigious development of a constantly growing population; in a Europe, or rather in a universe thus constituted, a policy of withdrawal or abstention is simply the high road to decadence! In our time nations are great only through the activity they deploy; it is not by spreading the peaceable light of their institutions . . . that they are great, in the present day.

Spreading light without acting, without taking part in the affairs of the world, keeping out of all European alliances and seeing as a trap, an adventure, all expansion into Africa or the Orient—for a great nation to live this way, believe me, is to abdicate and, in less time than you may think, to sink from the first rank to the third and fourth.

Critical Thinking Questions

1. How many different reasons or justifications (such as economic, cultural, or others) does Ferry give for French expansion?

2. What do you think Ferry means by the phrase "civilizing duty"?

3. What does Ferry appear to think is the difference between French colonialism and earlier Spanish colonialism?

Europeans Carve Up the African "Cake" at Berlin
(1885)

During 1884 to 1885, the major European powers met in Berlin and decided upon the following ground rules for the colonization of virtually the whole of Africa. From this conference also came many of the boundaries (and many of the problems) of current African states. No Africans were invited to participate in the carve-up of their continent.

Freedom of Trade to All Nations

ARTICLE I. The trade of all nations shall enjoy complete freedom....

No Taxes to Be Levied on Wares Imported (with Slight Exceptions)

ARTICLE III. Wares, of whatever origin, imported into these regions, under whatsoever flag, by sea or river, or overland, shall be subject to no other taxes than such as may be levied as fair compensation for expenditure in the interests of trade, and which for this reason must be equally borne by the subjects themselves and by foreigners of all nationalities.

No Import or Transit Duties to Be Levied

ARTICLE IV. Merchandise imported into these regions shall remain free from import and transit dues....

ARTICLE VI. *Provisions Relative to Protection of the Natives, of Missionaries and Travellers, as well as Relative to Religious Liberty*

Preservation and Improvement of Native Tribes; Slavery, and the Slave Trade

All the powers exercising sovereign rights or influence in the aforesaid territories bind themselves to watch over the preservation of the native tribes, and to care for the improvement of the conditions of their moral and material well-being, and to help in suppressing slavery, and especially the slave trade.

Religious and Other Institutions. Civilization of Natives

They shall, without distinction of creed or nation, protect and favour all religious, scientific, or charitable institutions, and undertakings created and organized for the above ends, or which aim at instructing the natives and bringing home to them the blessings of civilization.

Protection of Missionaries, Scientists, and Explorers

Christian missionaries, scientists, and explorers, with their followers, property, and collections, shall likewise be the objects of especial protection.

Excerpts from the General Appendices, Raymond Leslie Buell, *The Native Problem in Africa*, Macmillan Company, 1928.

Religious Toleration

Freedom of conscience and religious toleration are expressly guaranteed to the natives, no less than to subjects and to foreigners.

Public Worship

The free and public exercise of all forms of Divine worship, and the right to build edifices for religious purposes, and to organize religious missions belonging to all creeds, shall not be limited or fettered in any way whatsoever....

Suppression of the Slave Trade by Land and Sea; and of Slave Markets

ARTICLE IX. Seeing that trading in slaves is forbidden in conformity with the principles of international law as recognized by the Signatory Powers, and seeing also that the operations, which, by sea or land, furnish slaves to trade, ought likewise to be regarded as forbidden, the Powers which do or shall exercise sovereign rights or influence in the territories forming the Conventional basin of the Congo declare that these territories may not serve as a market or means of transit for the trade in slaves, of whatever race they may be. Each of the Powers binds itself to employ all means at its disposal for putting an end to this trade and for punishing those who engage in it....

Notification of Acquisitions and Protectorates on Coasts of African Continent

ARTICLE XXXIV. Any power which henceforth takes possession of a tract of land on the coasts of the African continent outside of its present possessions, or which, hitherto without such possessions, shall acquire them, as well as the Power which assumes a Protectorate there, shall accompany the respective act with a notification thereof, addressed to the other Signatory Powers of the present Act, in order to enable them, if need be, to make good any claims of their own.

Establishment of Authority in Territories Occupied on Coasts, Protection of Existing Rights, Freedom of Trade and Transit

ARTICLE XXXV. The Signatory Powers of the present Act recognize the obligation to insure the establishment of authority in regions occupied by them on the coasts of the African continent sufficient to protect existing rights, and, as the case may be, freedom of trade and of transit under the conditions agreed upon.

Critical Thinking Questions

1. What do you think was the main concern at the heart of this agreement?

2. Some Europeans justified their takeover of Africa as a benevolent act or "white man's burden"—done for the benefit of Africans themselves. What evidence can you cite from the document that suggests concern for African well-being? What evidence is there to the contrary?

Rudyard Kipling, The White Man's Burden
(1899)

Rudyard Kipling, a British poet and novelist, was a leading proponent of late nineteenth century "New Imperialism." The following poem, which was an appeal to the United States who had recently acquired the Philippines in the Spanish-American War, serves at least two functions: it expresses a popular notion of the nature and intent of British imperialism at the end of the nineteenth century, and it serves as a justification of imperialism.

Take up the White Man's burden—
Send forth the best ye breed—
Go bind your sons to exile
To serve your captives' need;
To wait in heavy harness,
On fluttered folk and wild—
Your new-caught, sullen peoples,
Half-devil and half-child.

Take up the White Man's burden—
In patience to abide,
To veil the threat of terror
And check the show of pride;
By open speech and simple,
An hundred times made plain
To seek another's profit,
And work another's gain.

Take up the White Man's burden—
The savage wars of peace—
Fill full the mouth of Famine
And bid the sickness cease;
And when your goal is nearest
The end for others sought,
Watch sloth and heathen Folly
Bring all your hopes to nought.

Take up the White Man's burden—
No tawdry rule of kings,
But toil of serf and sweeper—
The tale of common things.
The ports ye shall not enter,
The roads ye shall not tread,
Go mark them with your living,
And mark them with your dead.

Take up the White Man's burden—
And reap his old reward:
The blame of those ye better,
The hate of those ye guard—
The cry of hosts ye humour
(Ah, slowly!) toward the light:—
"Why brought he us from bondage,
Our loved Egyptian night?"

Take up the White Man's burden—
Ye dare not stoop to less—
Nor call too loud on Freedom

From *The White Man's Burden* by Rudyard Kipling, 1899.

To cloke your weariness;
By all ye cry or whisper,
By all ye leave or do,
The silent, sullen peoples
Shall weigh your gods and you.

Take up the White Man's burden—
Have done with childish days—
The lightly proferred laurel,

The easy, ungrudged praise.
Comes now, to search your manhood
Through all the thankless years
Cold, edged with dear-bought wisdom,
The judgment of your peers!

Critical Thinking Questions

1. What is the "white man's burden"? What responsibilities does a colonial power have toward its subjects?

2. What do you think Kipling meant by "the savage wars of peace" (verse 3, line 2)? What does this imply about the reactions of native peoples to imperialism?

3. How does Kipling view native peoples?

III. The Modern World, 1900-1945

The First World War

Vladimir Il'ich Lenin, What Is to Be Done? *(1902)*

Woodrow Wilson, Speech on the Fourteen Points (1918)

The Treaty of Versailles (1919)

Vladimir Il'ich Lenin, What Is to Be Done?
(1902)

Lenin was the leader of the 1917 Communist Revolution in Russia. The groundwork for that achievement, however, was laid much earlier, as this 1902 document suggests. Here, Lenin examines the nature of Marxist organization and the prospects for achieving a Communist revolution in the future, and adds some novel twists to Marx's original vision.

On questions both of organisation and of politics the Economists are forever lapsing from Social-Democracy into trade-unionism. The political struggle of Social-Democracy is far more extensive and complex than the economic struggle of the workers against the employers and the government. Similarly (indeed for that reason), the organisation of the revolutionary Social-Democratic Party must inevitably be of *a kind different* from the organisation of the workers designed for this struggle. The workers' organisation must in the first place be a trade-union organisation; secondly, it must be as broad as possible; and thirdly, it must be as public as conditions will allow (here, and further on, of course, I refer only to absolutist Russia). On the other hand, the organisation of the revolutionaries must consist first and foremost of people who make revolutionary activity their profession (for which reason I speak of the organisation of *revolutionaries*, meaning revolutionary Social-Democrats). In view of this common characteristic of the members of such an organisation, *all distinctions as between workers and intellectuals,* not to speak of distinctions of trade and profession, in both categories, *must be effaced.* Such an organisation must perforce not be very extensive and must be as secret as possible....

The workers' organisations for the economic struggle should be trade-union organisations. Every Social-Democratic worker should as far as possible assist and actively work in these organisations. But, while this is true, it is certainly not in our interest to demand that only Social-Democrats should be eligible for membership in the "trade" unions, since that would only narrow the scope of our influence upon the masses. Let every worker who understands the need to unite for the struggle against the employers and the government join the trade unions. The very aim of the trade unions would be impossible of achievement, if they did not unite all who have attained at least this elementary degree of understanding, if they were not very *broad* organisations. The broader these organisations, the broader will be our influence over them—an influence due, not only to the "spontaneous" development of the economic struggle, but to the direct and conscious effort of the socialist trade-union members to influence their comrades. But a broad organisation cannot apply methods of strict secrecy (since this demands far greater training than is required for the economic struggle). How is the contradiction between the need for a large membership and the

From *Collected Works,* Volume 5 by V.I. Lenin, Progress Publishers, Moscow.

need for strictly secret methods to be reconciled? How are we to make the trade unions as public as possible? Generally speaking, there can be only two ways to this end: either the trade unions become legalised (in some countries this preceded the legalisation of the socialist and political unions), or the organisation is kept secret, but so "free" and amorphous, *lose* as the Germans say, that the need for secret methods becomes almost negligible as far as the bulk of the members is concerned. . . .

I could go on analysing the Rules, but I think that what has been said will suffice. A small, compact core of the most reliable, experienced, and hardened workers, with responsible representatives in the principal districts and connected by all the rules of strict secrecy with the organisation of revolutionaries, can, with the widest support of the masses and without any formal organisation, perform *all* the functions of a trade-union organisation, in a manner, moreover, desirable to Social-Democracy. Only in this way can we secure the *consolidation* and development of a *Social-Democratic* trade-union movement, despite all the gendarmes.

It may be objected that an organisation which is so [*loose*] that it is not even definitely formed, and which has not even an enrolled and registered membership, cannot be called an organisation at all. Perhaps so. Not the name is important. What is important is that this "organisation without members" shall do everything that is required, and from the very outset ensure a solid connection between our future trade unions and socialism. Only an incorrigible utopian would have a *broad* organisation of workers, with elections, reports, universal suffrage, etc., under the autocracy.

The moral to be drawn from this is simple. If we begin with the solid foundation of a strong organisation of revolutionaries, we can ensure the stability of the movement as a whole and carry out the aims both of Social-Democracy and of trade unions proper. If, however, we begin with a broad workers' organisation, which is supposedly most "accessible" to the masses (but which is actually most accessible to the gendarmes and makes revolutionaries most accessible to the police), we shall achieve neither the one aim nor the other; we shall not eliminate our rule-of-thumb methods, and, because we remain scattered and our forces are constantly broken up by the police, we shall only make trade unions of the Zubatov and Ozerov type the more accessible to the masses.

Critical Thinking Questions

1. What is the basic problem that Lenin identifies and tries to address in this document?

2. In *The Communist Manifesto,* Marx spoke only of one agent of revolution—the proletariat (or factory working class). Does Lenin say the same thing or something different? Explain your answer.

3. Why, according to Lenin, should the revolutionary movement be centralized?

4. What do you think is the *one* passage that best captures the meaning of the whole document. Say why.

Woodrow Wilson, Speech on the Fourteen Points
(1918)

Woodrow Wilson (1856–1924) was the American president responsible for bringing the U. S. into World War I. In the following speech to Congress on January 8, 1918, Wilson outlined possible peace terms for ending the war and offered a plan for reconstructing a new Europe after the war. Wilson sincerely believed that the enactment of his "Fourteen Points", which include principles such as open covenants, self-determination, and the creation of the League of Nations, would form the basis of a just and lasting peace in Europe. Although these principles did become the basis for Germany's surrender in 1918, the U. S. Senate refused to ratify the Treaty of Versailles and the U. S. never joined the League of Nations.

We entered this war because violations of right had occurred which touched us to the quick and made the life of our own people impossible unless they were corrected and the world secured once for all against their recurrence. What we demand in this war, therefore, is nothing peculiar to ourselves. It is that the world be made fit and safe to live in; and particularly that it be made safe for every peaceloving nation which, like our own, wishes to live its own life, determine its own institutions, be assured of justice and fair dealing by the other peoples of the world as against force and selfish aggression. All the peoples of the world are in effect partners in this interest, and for our own part we see very clearly that unless justice be done to others it will not be done to us. The programme of the world's peace, therefore, is our programme; and that programme, the only possible programme, as we see it, is this:

I. Open covenants of peace, openly arrived at, after which there shall be no private international understanding of any kind but diplomacy shall proceed always frankly and in the public view.

II. Absolute freedom of navigation upon the seas, outside territorial waters, alike in peace and in war, except as the seas may be closed in whole or in part by international action for the enforcement of international covenants.

III. The removal, so far as possible, of all economic barriers and the establishment of an equality of trade conditions among all the nations consenting to the peace and associating themselves for its maintenance.

IV. Adequate guarantees given and taken that national armaments will be reduced to the lowest point consistent with domestic safety.

V. A free, openminded, and absolutely impartial adjustment of all colonial claims, based upon a strict observance of the principle that in determining all such questions of sovereignty the interests of the populations concerned must have equal weight with

---

Speech on the Fourteen Points, January 8, 1918, Woodrow Wilson.

the equitable claims of the government whose title is to be determined.

VI. The evacuation of all Russian territory and such a settlement of all questions affecting Russia as will secure the best and freest cooperation of the other nations of the world in obtaining for her an unhampered and unembarrassed opportunity for the independent determination of her own political development and national policy and assure her a sincere welcome into the society of free nations under institutions of her own choosing; and, more than a welcome, assistance also of every kind that she may need and may herself desire. The treatment accorded Russia by her sister nations in the months to come will be the acid test of their good will, of their comprehension of her needs as distinguished from their own interests, and of their intelligent and unselfish sympathy.

VII. Belgium, the whole world will agree, must be evacuated and restored, without any attempt to limit the sovereignty which she enjoys in common with all other free nations. No other single act will serve as this will serve to restore confidence among the nations in the laws which they have themselves set and determined for the government of their relations with one another. Without this healing act the whole structure and validity of international law is forever impaired.

VIII. All French territory should be freed and the invaded portions restored, and the wrong done to France by Prussia in 1871 in the matter of Alsace-Lorraine, which has unsettled the peace of the world for nearly fifty years, should be righted, in order that peace may once more be made secure in the interest of all.

IX. A readjustment of the frontiers of Italy should be effected along clearly recognizable lines of nationality.

X. The peoples of Austria-Hungary, whose place among the nations we wish to see safeguarded and assured, should be accorded the freest opportunity of autonomous development.

XI. Rumania, Serbia, and Montenegro should be evacuated; occupied territories restored; Serbia accorded free and secure access to the sea; and the relations of the several Balkan states to one another determined by friendly counsel along historically established lines of allegiance and nationality; and international guarantees of the political and economic independence and territorial integrity of the several Balkan states should be entered into.

XII. The Turkish portions of the present Ottoman Empire should be assured a secure sovereignty, but the other nationalities which are now under Turkish rule should be assured an undoubted security of life and an absolutely unmolested opportunity of autonomous development, and the Dardanelles should be permanently opened as a free passage to the ships and commerce of all nations under international guarantees.

XIII. An independent Polish state should be erected which should include the territories inhabited by indisputably Polish populations, which should be assured a free and secure access to the sea, and whose political and economic independence and territorial integrity should be guaranteed by international covenant.

XIV. A general association of nations must be formed under specific covenants for the purpose of affording mutual guarantees of political independence and territorial integrity to great and small states alike....

From Woodrow Wilson, "Speech on the Fourteen Points," *Congressional Record*, 65th Congress 2nd Session, 1918, pp. 680–681.

Critical Thinking Questions

1. Many of Wilson's "Fourteen Points" were an attempt to prevent the repetition of World War I. Which articles were a direct response to the causes of World War I or to events that occurred during the war?

2. According to Wilson, what should be the guiding principle behind the territorial changes that occur after World War I? Who should have the greatest role in deciding questions of national borders?

3. What is the "general association of nations" to which Wilson refers in point XIV? What was the purpose of this association?

4. Why do you think the other Allied Powers, particularly France, rejected Wilson's Fourteen Points as the basis for Germany's peace treaty?

The Treaty of Versailles
(1919)

The Treaty of Versailles (signed on June 28, 1919) officially ended hostilities between Germany and the Western Allies. The document represented British and French efforts both to punish Germany and to ensure that it could never again become a threat to its neighbors.

The Terms of the Treaty of Versailles

Part IV
German Rights and Interests Outside Germany

ARTICLE 119

Germany renounces in favour of the Principal Allied and Associated Powers all her rights and titles over her oversea possessions.

Part V
Military, Naval and Air Clauses

In order to render possible the initiation of a general limitation of the armaments of all nations, Germany undertakes strictly to observe the military, naval and air clauses which follow.

ARTICLE 160

(1) By a date which must not be later than March 31, 1920, the German Army must not comprise more than seven divisions of infantry and three divisions of cavalry.

After that date the total number of effectives in the Army of the States constituting Germany must not exceed one hundred thousand men, including officers and establishments of depots. The Army shall be devoted exclusively to the maintenance of order within the territory and to the control of the frontiers.

The total effective strength of officers, including the personnel of staffs, whatever their composition, must not exceed four thousand.

ARTICLE 178

All measures of mobilisation or appertaining to mobilisation are forbidden.

In no case must formations, administrative services or General Staffs include supplementary cadres.

ARTICLE 180

All fortified works, fortresses and field works situated in German territory to the west of a line drawn fifty kilometres to the east of the Rhine shall be disarmed and dismantled.

ARTICLE 181

After the expiration of a period of two months from the coming into force of the present Treaty the German naval forces in commission must not exceed:

6 battleships of the *Deutschland* or *Lothringen* type,
6 light cruisers,
12 destroyers,
12 torpedo boats,

From *The Treaties of Peace*, 1919–1923. Volume 1, (New York: Carnegie Endowment for International Peace, 1924).

or an equal number of ships constructed to replace them as provided in Article 190.

No submarines are to be included.

All other warships, except where there is provision to the contrary in the present Treaty, must be placed in reserve or devoted to commercial purposes.

ARTICLE 183

After the expiration of a period of two months from the coming into force of the present Treaty, the total personnel of the German Navy, including the manning of the fleet, coast defences, signal stations, administration and other land services, must not exceed fifteen thousand, including officers and men of all grades and corps.

The total strength of officers and warrant officers must not exceed fifteen hundred.

Within two months from the coming into force of the present Treaty the personnel in excess of the above strength shall be demobilised.

No naval or military corps or reserve force in connection with the Navy may be organised in Germany without being included in the above strength.

ARTICLE 198

The armed forces of Germany must not include any military or naval air forces.

ARTICLE 199

Within two months from the coming into force of the present Treaty the personnel of air forces on the rolls of the German land and sea forces shall be demobilised.

ARTICLE 201

During the six months following the coming into force of the present Treaty, the manufacture and importation of aircraft, parts of aircraft, engines for aircraft, and parts of engines for aircraft, shall be forbidden in all German territory.

Part VIII
Reparation
Section I
General Provisions

ARTICLE 231

The Allied and Associated Governments affirm and Germany accepts the responsibility of Germany and her allies for causing all the loss and damage to which the Allied and Associated Governments and their nationals have been subjected as a consequence of the war imposed upon them by the aggression of Germany and her allies.

Critical Thinking Questions

1. Which article do you think was most clearly "punitive" (rather than simply an effort to prevent future German aggression)? Why?

2. Reduce article 231 to a single, clear sentence. What kinds of further actions against Germany can you imagine *might* have been made possible by German acceptance of this article?

3. Do you think this was a fair treaty to impose on Germany? Why or why not?

Dictatorship & the Second World War

The Program of the German Workers' Party (1920)

Adolf Hitler on "Nation and Race" (1925)

A. O. Avdienko Praises Stalin (1935)

Elie Wiesel, Night

The Program of the German Workers' Party
(1920)

Adolf Hitler cowrote and presented the following political "program" at a meeting of the German Workers' Party on February 24, 1920. Two months later the Party, which Hitler already lead, changed its name to the National Socialist German Workers' Party, or Nazi Party for short.

The National Socialist German Workers' Party at a great mass-meeting on February 25th, 1920, in the Hofbräuhaus-Festsaal in Munich announced their Programme to the world.

In section 2 of the Constitution of our Party this Programme is declared to be inalterable.

The Programme

The Programme of the German Workers' Party is limited as to period. The leaders have no intention, once the aims announced in it have been achieved, of setting up fresh ones, merely in order to increase the discontent of the masses artificially, and so ensure the continued existence of the Party.

1. We demand the union of all Germans to form a Great Germany on the basis of the right of the self-determination enjoyed by nations.

2. We demand equality of rights for the German People in its dealings with other nations, and abolition of the Peace Treaties of Versailles and St. Germain.

3. We demand land and territory (colonies) for the nourishment of our people and for settling our superfluous population.

4. None but members of the nation may be citizens of the State. None but those of German blood, whatever their creed, may be members of the nation. No Jew, therefore, may be a member of the nation.

5. Anyone who is not a citizen of the State may live in Germany only as a guest and must be regarded as being subject to foreign laws.

6. The right of voting on the State's government and legislation is to be enjoyed by the citizen of the State alone. We demand therefore that all official appointments, of whatever kind, whether in the Reich, in the country, or in the smaller localities, shall be granted to citizens of the State alone.

We oppose the corrupting custom of Parliament of filling posts merely with a view to party considerations, and without reference to character or capability.

7. We demand that the State shall make it its first duty to promote the industry and livelihood of citizens of the State. If it is not possible to nourish the entire population of the State, foreign nationals (non-citizens of the State) must be excluded from the Reich.

8. All non-German immigration must be prevented. We demand that all non-Germans, who

---

From *The Programme of the Party of Hitler*, translated by F.T.S. Dugdale, US Department of State.

entered Germany subsequent to August 2nd, 1914, shall be required forthwith to depart from the Reich.

9. All citizens of the State shall be equal as regards rights and duties.

10. It must be the first duty of each citizen of the State to work with his mind or with his body. The activities of the individual may not clash with the interests of the whole, but must proceed within the frame of the community and be for the general good.

We demand therefore:

11. Abolition of incomes unearned by work.

Abolition of the Thraldom of Interest

12. In view of the enormous sacrifice of life and property demanded of a nation by every war, personal enrichment due to a war must be regarded as a crime against the nation. We demand therefore ruthless confiscation of all war gains.

13. We demand nationalization of all businesses which have been up to the present formed into companies (Trusts).

14. We demand that the profits from wholesale trade shall be shared out.

15. We demand extensive development of provision for old age.

16. We demand creation and maintenance of a healthy middle class, immediate communalisation of wholesale business premises, and their lease at a cheap rate to small traders, and that extreme consideration shall be shown to all small purveyors to the State, district authorities and smaller localities.

17. We demand land-reform suitable to our national requirements, passing of a law for confiscation without compensation of land for communal purposes; abolition of interest on land loans, and prevention of all speculation in land.

18. We demand ruthless prosecution of those whose activities are injurious to the common interest. Sordid criminals against the nation, usurers, profiteers, etc. must be punished with death, whatever their creed or race.

19. We demand that the Roman Law, which serves the materialistic world order, shall be replaced by a legal system for all Germany.

20. With the aim of opening to every capable and industrious German the possibility of higher education and of thus obtaining advancement, the State must consider a thorough reconstruction of our national system of education. The curriculum of all educational establishments must be brought into line with the requirements of practical life. Comprehension of the State idea (State sociology) must be the school objective, beginning with the first dawn of intelligence in the pupil. We demand development of the gifted children of poor parents, whatever their class or occupation, at the expense of the State.

21. The State must see to raising the standard of health in the nation by protecting mothers and infants, prohibiting child labour, increasing bodily efficiency by obligatory gymnastics and sports laid down by law, and by extensive support of clubs engaged in the bodily development of the young.

22. We demand abolition of a paid army and formation of a national army.

23. We demand legal warfare against conscious political lying and its dissemination in the Press. In order to facilitate creation of a German national Press we demand:

(a) that all editors of newspapers and their assistants, employing the German language, must be members of the nation;

(b) that special permission from the State shall be necessary before non-German newspapers may appear. These are not necessarily printed in the German language;

(c) that non-Germans shall be prohibited by law from participation financially in or influencing German newspapers, and that the penalty for contravention of the law shall be suppression of any such newspaper, and immediate deportation of the non-German concerned in it.

It must be forbidden to publish papers which do not conduce to the national welfare. We demand legal prosecution of all tendencies in art and literature of a kind likely to disintegrate our life as a nation, and the suppression of institutions which militate against the requirements above-mentioned.

24. We demand liberty for all religious denominations in the State, so far as they are not a danger to it and do not militate against the moral feelings of the German race.

The Party, as such, stands for positive Christianity, but does not bind itself in the matter of creed to any particular confession. It combats the Jewish-materialist spirit within us and without us, and is convinced that our nation can only achieve permanent health from within on the principle:

The Common Interest Before Self

25. That all the foregoing may be realised we demand the creation of a strong central power of the State. Unquestioned authority of the politically centralized Parliament over the entire Reich and its organizations; and formation of Chambers for classes and occupations for the purpose of carrying out the general laws promulgated by the Reich in the various States of the confederation.

The leaders of the Party swear to go straight forward—if necessary to sacrifice their lives—in securing fulfilment of the foregoing Points.

Munich, February 24th, 1920.

Critical Thinking Questions

1. What do you think is the point of the preamble to article 1 ("The Programme")?

2. Identify those articles which reflect "nationalist," "socialist," and "racialist" or "anti-Semitic" ideals. Remember, some clauses may reflect multiple ideals.

3. To whom do you think this document was addressed? What group(s) did the Nazis hope to attract with this program?

4. Which *one* article do you think best represents the essence of the Party program overall? Justify your answer.

Adolf Hitler on "Nation and Race"
(1925)

During 1924, while serving a prison sentence for his effort to overthrow the government in Bavaria, Hitler wrote his autobiography, Mein Kampf. *The book's notions about nation and race, which are excerpted here, were not subsequently altered in any significant way either by Hitler himself or by other Nazi writers.*

Hitler's *Mein Kampf:* Nation and Race

Even the most superficial observation shows that Nature's restricted form of propagation and increase is an almost rigid basic law of all the innumerable forms of expression of her vital urge. Every animal mates only with a member of the same species. The titmouse seeks the titmouse, the finch the finch, the stork the stork, the field mouse the field mouse, the dormouse the dormouse, the wolf the she-wolf, etc.

Only unusual circumstances can change this, primarily the compulsion of captivity or any other cause that makes it impossible to mate within the same species. But then Nature begins to resist this with all possible means, and her most visible protest consists either in refusing further capacity for propagation to bastards or in limiting the fertility of later offspring; in most cases, however, she takes away the power of resistance to disease or hostile attacks.

This is only too natural.

Any crossing of two beings not at exactly the same level produces a medium between the level of the two parents. This means: the offspring will probably stand higher than the racially lower parent, but not as high as the higher one. Consequently, it will later succumb in the struggle against the higher level. Such mating is contrary to the will of Nature for a higher breeding of all life. The precondition for this does not lie in associating superior and inferior, but in the total victory of the former. The stronger must dominate and not blend with the weaker, thus sacrificing his own greatness. Only the born weakling can view this as cruel, but he after all is only a weak and limited man; for if this law did not prevail, any conceivable higher development of organic living beings would be unthinkable.

The consequence of this racial purity, universally valid in Nature, is not only the sharp outward delimitation of the various races, but their uniform character in themselves. The fox is always a fox, the goose a goose, the tiger a tiger, etc., and the difference can lie at most in the varying measure of force, strength, intelligence, dexterity, endurance, etc., of the individual specimens. But you will never find a fox who in his inner attitude might, for example, show humanitarian tendencies toward geese, as similarly there is no cat with a friendly inclination toward mice....

If the process were different, all further and higher development would cease and the opposite would occur. For, since the inferior always predominates numerically over the best, if both had the same possibility of preserving life and propagating, the inferior would multiply so much more rapidly

---

Excerpts from *Mein Kampf* by Adolf Hitler, translated by Ralph Manheim. Copyright © 1943, renewed 1971 by Houghton Mifflin Company. Reprinted by permission of Houghton Mifflin Company. All rights reserved.

that in the end the best would inevitably be driven into the background, unless a correction of this state of affairs were undertaken. Nature does just this by subjecting the weaker part to such severe living conditions that by them alone the number is limited, and by not permitting the remainder to increase promiscuously, but making a new and ruthless choice according to strength and health.

No more than Nature desires the mating of weaker with stronger individuals, even less does she desire the blending of a higher with a lower race, since, if she did, her whole work of higher breeding, over perhaps hundreds of thousands of years, might be ruined with one blow.

Historical experience offers countless proofs of this. It shows with terrifying clarity that in every mingling of Aryan blood with that of lower peoples the result was the end of the cultured people. North America, whose population consists in by far the largest part of Germanic elements who mixed but little with the lower colored peoples, shows a different humanity and culture from Central and South America, where the predominantly Latin immigrants often mixed with the aborigines on a large scale. By this one example, we can clearly and distinctly recognize the effect of racial mixture. The Germanic inhabitant of the American continent, who has remained racially pure and unmixed, rose to be master of the continent; he will remain the master as long as he does not fall a victim to defilement of the blood.

The result of all racial crossing is therefore in brief always the following:

a. Lowering of the level of the higher race;
b. Physical and intellectual regression and hence the beginning of a slowly but surely progressing sickness.

To bring about such a development is, then, nothing else but to sin against the will of the eternal creator.

And as a sin this act is rewarded.

When man attempts to rebel against the iron logic of Nature, he comes into struggle with the principles to which he himself owes his existence as a man. And this attack must lead to his own doom.

Here, of course, we encounter the objection of the modern pacifist, as truly Jewish in its effrontery as it is stupid! "Man's role is to overcome Nature!"

Millions thoughtlessly parrot this Jewish nonsense and end up by really imagining that they themselves represent a kind of conqueror of Nature; though in this they dispose of no other weapon than an idea, and at that such a miserable one, that if it were true no world at all would be conceivable....

Everything we admire on this earth today—science and art, technology and inventions—is only the creative product of a few peoples and originally perhaps of *one* race. On them depends the existence of this whole culture. If they perish, the beauty of this earth will sink into the grave with them....

All great cultures of the past perished only because the originally creative race died out from blood poisoning.

The ultimate cause of such a decline was their forgetting that all culture depends on men and not conversely; hence that to preserve a certain culture the man who creates it must be preserved. This preservation is bound up with the rigid law of necessity and the right to victory of the best and stronger in this world.

Those who want to live, let them fight, and those who do not want to fight in this world of eternal struggle do not deserve to live....

It is idle to argue which race or races were the original representative of human culture and hence the real founders of all that we sum up under the word "humanity." It is simpler to raise the question with regard to the present, and here an easy, clear answer results. All the human culture, all the results of art, science, and technology that we see before us today, are almost exclusively the creative product of the Aryan. This very fact admits of the not unfounded inference that he alone was the founder of all higher humanity, therefore representing the prototype of all that we understand by the word "man." He is the Prometheus of mankind from whose bright forehead the divine spark of genius has sprung at all times, forever kindling anew that fire of knowledge which illumined the night of silent mysteries and thus caused man to climb the path to mastery over the other beings of this earth. Exclude him—and perhaps after a few thousand years darkness will again descend on the earth, human culture will pass, and the world turn to a desert....

The mightiest counterpart to the Aryan is represented by the Jew. In hardly any people in the world is the instinct of self-preservation developed more strongly than in the so-called "chosen." Of this, the mere fact of the survival of this race may be considered the best proof. Where is the people which in the last two thousand years has been exposed to so slight changes of inner disposition, character, etc., as the Jewish people? What people, finally, has gone through greater upheavals than this one—and nevertheless issued from the mightiest catastrophes of mankind unchanged? What an infinitely tough will to live and preserve the species speaks from these facts!

The mental qualities of the Jew have been schooled in the course of many centuries. Today he passes as "smart," and this in a certain sense he has been at all times. But his intelligence is not the result of his own development, but of visual instruction through foreigners. For the human mind cannot climb to the top without steps; for every step upward he needs the foundation of the past, and this in the comprehensive sense in which it can be revealed only in general culture. All thinking is based only in small part on man's own knowledge, and mostly on the experience of the time that has preceded. The general cultural level provides the individual man, without his noticing it as a rule, with such a profusion of preliminary knowledge that, thus armed, he can more easily take further steps of his own. The boy of today, for example, grows up among a truly vast number of technical acquisitions of the last centuries, so that he takes for granted and no longer pays attention to much that a hundred years ago was a riddle to even the greatest minds, although for following and understanding our progress in the field in question it is of decisive importance to him. If a very genius from the twenties of the past century should suddenly leave his grave today, it would be harder for him even intellectually to find his way in the present era than for an average boy of fifteen today. For he would lack all the infinite preliminary education which our present contemporary unconsciously, so to speak, assimilates while growing up amidst the manifestations of our present general civilization.

Since the Jew—for reasons which will at once become apparent—was never in possession of a culture of his own, the foundations of his intellectual work were always provided by others. His intellect at all times developed through the cultural world surrounding him.

The reverse process never took place.

For if the Jewish people's instinct of self-preservation is not smaller but larger than that of other peoples, if his intellectual faculties can easily arouse the impression that they are equal to the intellectual gifts of other races, he lacks completely the most essential requirement for a cultured people, the idealistic attitude.

In the Jewish people the will to self-sacrifice does not go beyond the individual's naked instinct of self-preservation. Their apparently great sense of solidarity is based on the very primitive herd instinct that is seen in many other living creatures in this world. It is a noteworthy fact that the herd instinct leads to mutual support only as long as a common danger makes this seem useful or inevitable. The same pack of wolves which has just fallen on its prey together disintegrates when hunger abates into its individual beasts. The same is true of horses which try to defend themselves against an assailant in a body, but scatter again as soon as the danger is past.

It is similar with the Jew. His sense of sacrifice is only apparent. It exists only as long as the existence of the individual makes it absolutely necessary. However, as soon as the common enemy is conquered, the danger threatening all averted and the booty hidden, the apparent harmony of the Jews among themselves ceases, again making way for their old causal tendencies. The Jew is only united when a common danger forces him to be or a common booty entices him; if these two grounds are lacking, the qualities of the crassest egoism come into their own, and in the twinkling of an eye the united people turns into a horde of rats, fighting bloodily among themselves.

If the Jews were alone in this world, they would stifle in filth and offal; they would try to get ahead of one another in hate-filled struggle and exterminate one another, in so far as the absolute absence of all sense of self-sacrifice, expressing itself in their cowardice, did not turn battle into comedy here too.

So it is absolutely wrong to infer any ideal sense of sacrifice in the Jews from the fact that they stand together in struggle, or, better expressed, in the plundering of their fellow men.

Here again the Jew is led by nothing but the naked egoism of the individual.

That is why the Jewish state—which should be the living organism for preserving and increasing a race—is completely unlimited as to territory. For a state formation to have a definite spatial setting always presupposes an idealistic attitude on the part of the state-race, and especially a correct interpretation of the concept of work. In the exact measure in which this attitude is lacking, any attempt at forming, even of preserving, a spatially delimited state fails. And thus the basis on which alone culture can arise is lacking.

Hence the Jewish people, despite all apparent intellectual qualities, is without any true culture, and especially without any culture of its own. For what sham culture the Jew today possesses is the property of other peoples, and for the most part it is ruined in his hands.

In judging the Jewish people's attitude on the question of human culture, the most essential characteristic we must always bear in mind is that there has never been a Jewish art and accordingly there is none today either; that above all the two queens of all the arts, architecture and music, owe nothing original to the Jews. What they do accomplish in the field of art is either patchwork or intellectual theft. Thus, the Jew lacks those qualities which distinguish the races that are creative and hence culturally blessed.

To what an extent the Jew takes over foreign culture, imitating or rather ruining it, can be seen from the fact that he is mostly found in the art which seems to require least original invention, the art of acting. But even here, in reality, he is only a "juggler," or rather an ape; for even here he lacks the last touch that is required for real greatness; even here he is not the creative genius, but a superficial imitator, and all the twists and tricks that he uses are powerless to conceal the inner lifelessness of his creative gift. Here the Jewish press most lovingly helps him along by raising such a roar of hosannahs about even the most mediocre bungler, just so long as he is a Jew, that the rest of the world actually ends up by thinking that they have an artist before them, while in truth it is only a pitiful comedian.

No, the Jew possesses no culture-creating force of any sort, since the idealism, without which there is no true higher development of man, is not present in him and never was present. Hence his intellect will never have a constructive effect, but will be destructive, and in very rare cases perhaps will at most be stimulating, but then as the prototype of the "force which always wants evil and nevertheless creates good."[1] Not through him does any progress of mankind occur, but in spite of him....

The Jew's life as a parasite in the body of other nations and states explains a characteristic which once caused Schopenhauer, as has already been mentioned, to call him the "great master in lying." Existence impels the Jew to lie, and to lie perpetually, just as it compels the inhabitants of the northern countries to wear warm clothing.

His life within other peoples can only endure for any length of time if he succeeds in arousing the opinion that he is not a people but a "religious community," though of a special sort.

And this is the first great lie.

In order to carry on his existence as a parasite on other peoples, he is forced to deny his inner nature. The more intelligent the individual Jew is, the more he will succeed in this deception. Indeed, things can go so far that large parts of the host people will end by seriously believing that the Jew is really a Frenchman or an Englishman, a German or an Italian, though of a special religious faith. Especially state authorities, which always seem animated by the historical fraction of wisdom, most easily fall a victim to this infinite deception. Independent thinking sometimes seems to these circles a true sin against holy advancement, so that we may not be surprised if even today a Bavarian state ministry, for example, still has not the faintest idea that the Jews are members of a *people* and not of a *"religion"* though a glance at the Jew's own newspapers should indicate this even to the most modest mind. The *Jewish Echo* is not yet an official organ, of course, and consequently is unauthoritative as far as the intelligence of one of these government potentates is concerned.

The Jew has always been a people with definite racial characteristics and never a religion; only in order to get ahead he early sought for a means which could distract unpleasant attention from his person. And what would have been more expedient and at the same time more innocent than the "embezzled" concept of a religious community? For here, too, everything is borrowed or rather stolen. Due to his own original special nature, the Jew cannot possess a religious institution, if for no other reason because he lacks idealism in any form, and hence belief in a hereafter is absolutely foreign to him. And a religion in the Aryan sense cannot be imagined which lacks the conviction of survival after death in some form. Indeed, the Talmud is not a book to prepare a man for the hereafter, but only for a practical and profitable life in this world.

The Jewish religious doctrine consists primarily in prescriptions for keeping the blood of Jewry pure and for regulating the relation of Jews among themselves, but even more with the rest of the world; in other words, with non-Jews. But even here it is by no means ethical problems that are involved, but extremely modest economic ones. Concerning the moral value of Jewish religious instruction, there are today and have been at all times rather exhaustive studies (not by Jews; the drivel of the Jews themselves on the subject is, of course, adapted to its purpose) which make this kind of religion seem positively monstrous according to Aryan conceptions. The best characterization is provided by the product of this religious education, the Jew himself. His life is only of this world, and his spirit is inwardly as alien to true Christianity as his nature two thousand years previous was to the great founder of the new doctrine. Of course, the latter made no secret of his attitude toward the Jewish people, and when necessary he even took to the whip to drive from the temple of the Lord this adversary of all humanity, who then as always saw in religion nothing but an instrument for his business existence. In return, Christ was nailed to the cross, while our present-day party Christians debase themselves to begging for Jewish votes at elections and later try to arrange political swindles with atheistic Jewish parties—and this against their own nation.

On this first and greatest lie, that the Jews are not a race but a religion, more and more lies are based in necessary consequence. Among them is the lie with regard to the language of the Jew. For him it is not a means for expressing his thoughts, but a means for concealing them. When he speaks French, he thinks Jewish, and while he turns out German verses, in his life he only expresses the nature of his nationality. As long as the Jew has not become the master of the other peoples, he must speak their languages whether he likes it or not, but as soon as they became his slaves, they would all have to learn a universal language (Esperanto, for instance!) so that by this additional means the Jews could more easily dominate them!

---

[1] Goethe's *Faust*, lines 1336–1337: Mephistopheles to Faust.

Critical Thinking Questions

1. What do Hitler's comments about "titmice," "finches," "wolves," etc. (at the beginning of the reading), tell us about his thoughts on human "racial" identities? On what grounds does Hitler oppose racial mixing?

2. Find the part of the reading where Hitler discusses the racial histories of North, Central, and South America. What does he argue? What is the basic problem with his logic and assumptions?

3. According to Hitler, what are the defining characteristics of "Aryans" and Jews?

4. What does Hitler argue is the "first great lie" of the Jews? Why might this distinction be significant to Hitler?

A. O. Avdienko Praises Stalin
(1935)

Stalin became Communist Party general secretary in 1922. He used this position to outmaneuver his rivals in the struggle for power that followed Lenin's death in 1924, after which time he began to build a massive cult of personality that peaked after World War II. The following speech—by writer A. O. Avdienko and given in February 1935 before the Seventh Congress of Soviets—was typical of the kind of praise lavished on the "Great Leader." Stalin ruled the Soviet Union absolutely until his death in 1953.

Thank you, Stalin. Thank you because I am joyful. Thank you because I am well. No matter how old I become, I shall never forget how we received Stalin two days ago. Centuries will pass, and the generations still to come will regard us as the happiest of mortals, as the most fortunate of men, because we lived in the century of centuries, because we were privileged to see Stalin, our inspired leader. Yes, and we regard ourselves as the happiest of mortals because we are the contemporaries of a man who never had an equal in world history.

The men of all ages will call on thy name, which is strong, beautiful, wise and marvellous. Thy name is engraven on every factory, every machine, every place on the earth, and in the hearts of all men.

Every time I have found myself in his presence I have been subjugated by his strength, his charm, his grandeur. I have experienced a great desire to sing, to cry out, to shout with joy and happiness. And now see me—me!—on the same platform where the Great Stalin stood a year ago. In what country, in what part of the world could such a thing happen?

I write books. I am an author. All thanks to thee, O great educator, Stalin. I love a young woman with a renewed love and shall perpetuate myself in my children—all thanks to thee, great educator, Stalin. I shall be eternally happy and joyous, all thanks to thee, great educator, Stalin. Everything belongs to thee, chief of our great country. And when the woman I love presents me with a child the first word it shall utter will be: Stalin.

O great Stalin, O leader of the peoples,
Thou who broughtest man to birth.
Thou who fructifiest the earth,
Thou who restorest the centuries,
Thou who makest bloom the spring,
Thou who makest vibrate the musical chords...
Thou, splendour of my spring, O Thou,
Sun reflected by millions of hearts...

From *Pravda*, February 1, 1935.

Critical Thinking Questions

1. What can be <u>inferred</u> from the speech about everyday life in the Soviet Union at the time?

2. What do you think is the point of the poem at the end? What does it say or express?

Elie Wiesel, Night

Holocaust survivor, Eliezer Wiesel (Elie for short), was originally born in the Jewish village of Sighet, Romania, in 1928. When Nazis took control of Sighet in 1944, Elie and his family were deported to concentration camps at Auschwitz and at Buna in Poland, before he was finally liberated by the U. S. Army in April 1945. In his most famous memoir, Night, *Wiesel describes his horrific experience as a Jewish prisoner in the Nazi death camps. After losing both of his parents, a sister, and most of his youth in the Holocaust, Wiesel has become a champion of human rights throughout the world.*

[At this point in the story, Elie and his family have arrived by train at Auschwitz, in Poland.]

THE BELOVED OBJECTS that we had carried with us from place to place were now left behind in the wagon and, with them, finally, our illusions.

Every few yards, there stood an SS man, his machine gun trained on us. Hand in hand we followed the throng.

An SS came toward us wielding a club. He commanded:

"Men to the left! Women to the right!"

Eight words spoken quietly, indifferently, without emotion. Eight simple, short words. Yet that was the moment when I left my mother. There was no time to think, and I already felt my father's hand press against mine: we were alone. In a fraction of a second I could see my mother, my sisters, move to the right. Tzipora was holding Mother's hand. I saw them walking farther and farther away; Mother was stroking my sister's blond hair, as if to protect her. And I walked on with my father, with the men. I didn't know that this was the moment in time and the place where I was leaving my mother and Tzipora forever. I kept walking, my father holding my hand.

Behind me, an old man fell to the ground. Nearby, an SS man replaced his revolver in its holster.

My hand tightened its grip on my father. All I could think of was not to lose him. Not to remain alone.

The SS officers gave the order.

"Form ranks of fives!"

There was a tumult. It was imperative to stay together.

"Hey, kid, how old are you?"

The man interrogating me was an inmate. I could not see his face, but his voice was weary and warm.

"Fifteen."

"No. You're eighteen."

"But I'm not," I said. "I'm fifteen."

"Fool. Listen to what *I* say."

Then he asked my father, who answered:

"I'm fifty."

"No." The man now sounded angry. "Not fifty. You're forty. Do you hear? Eighteen and forty."

He disappeared into the darkness. Another inmate appeared, unleashing a stream of invectives:

"Sons of bitches, why have you come here? Tell me, why?"

Someone dared to reply:

Excerpt from NIGHT by Elie Wiesel, translation by Marion Wiesel. Translation copyright © 2006 by Marion Wiesel. Reprinted by permission of Hill and Wang, a division of Farrar, Straus and Giroux, LLC.

"What do you think? That we came here of our own free will? That we asked to come here?"

The other seemed ready to kill him:

"Shut up, you moron, or I'll tear you to pieces! You should have hanged yourselves rather than come here. Didn't you know what was in store for you here in Auschwitz? You didn't know? In 1944?"

True. We didn't know. Nobody had told us. He couldn't believe his ears. His tone became even harsher:

"Over there. Do you see the chimney over there? Do you see it? And the flames, do you see them?" (Yes, we saw the flames.) "Over there, that's where they will take you. Over there will be your grave. You still don't understand? You sons of bitches. Don't you understand anything? You will be burned! Burned to a cinder! Turned into ashes!"

His anger changed into fury. We stood stunned, petrified. Could this be just a nightmare? An unimaginable nightmare?

I heard whispers around me:

"We must do something. We can't let them kill us like that, like cattle in the slaughterhouse. We must revolt."

There were, among us, a few tough young men. They actually had knives and were urging us to attack the armed guards. One of them was muttering:

"Let the world learn about the existence of Auschwitz. Let everybody find out about it while they still have a chance to escape..."

But the older men begged their sons not to be foolish:

"We mustn't give up hope, even now as the sword hangs over our heads. So taught our sages..."

The wind of revolt died down. We continued to walk until we came to a crossroads. Standing in the middle of it was, though I didn't know it then, Dr. Mengele, the notorious Dr. Mengele. He looked like the typical SS officer: a cruel, though not unintelligent, face, complete with monocle. He was holding a conductor's baton and was surrounded by officers. The baton was moving constantly, sometimes to the right, sometimes to the left.

In no time, I stood before him.

"Your age?" he asked, perhaps trying to sound paternal.

"I'm eighteen." My voice was trembling.

"In good health?"

"Yes."

"Your profession?"

Tell him that I was a student?

"Farmer," I heard myself saying.

This conversation lasted no more than a few seconds. It seemed like an eternity.

The baton pointed to the left. I took half a step forward. I first wanted to see where they would send my father. Were he to have gone to the right, I would have run after him.

The baton, once more, moved to the left. A weight lifted from my heart.

We did not know, as yet, which was the better side, right or left, which road led to prison and which to the crematoria. Still, I was happy, I was near my father. Our procession continued slowly to move forward.

Another inmate came over to us:

"Satisfied?"

"Yes," someone answered.

"Poor devils, you are heading for the crematorium."

He seemed to be telling the truth. Not far from us, flames, huge flames, were rising from a ditch. Something was being burned there. A truck drew close and unloaded its hold: small children. Babies! Yes, I did see this, with my own eyes . . . children thrown into the flames. (Is it any wonder that ever since then, sleep tends to elude me?)

So that was where we were going. A little farther on, there was another, larger pit for adults.

I pinched myself: Was I still alive? Was I awake? How was it possible that men, women, and children were being burned and that the world kept silent? No. All this could not be real. A nightmare perhaps . . . Soon I would wake up with a start, my heart pounding, and find that I was back in the room of my childhood, with my books . . .

My father's voice tore me from my daydreams:

"What a shame, a shame that you did not go with your mother . . . I saw many children your age go with their mothers . . ."

His voice was terribly sad. I understood that he did not wish to see what they would do to me. He did not wish to see his only son go up in flames.

My forehead was covered with cold sweat. Still, I told him that I could not believe that human beings were being burned in our times; the world would never tolerate such crimes . . .

"The world? The world is not interested in us. Today, everything is possible, even the crematoria..." His voice broke.

"Father," I said. "If that is true, then I don't want to wait. I'll run into the electrified barbed wire. That would be easier than a slow death in the flames."

He didn't answer. He was weeping. His body was shaking. Everybody around us was weeping. Someone began to recite Kaddish, the prayer for the dead. I don't know whether, during the history of the Jewish people, men have ever before recited Kaddish for themselves.

"*Yisgadal, veyiskadash, shmey raba* . . . May His name be celebrated and sanctified . . ." whispered my father.

For the first time, I felt anger rising within me. Why should I sanctify His name? The Almighty, the eternal and terrible Master of the Universe, chose to be silent. What was there to thank Him for?

We continued our march. We were coming closer and closer to the pit, from which an infernal heat was rising. Twenty more steps. If I was going to kill myself, this was the time. Our column had only some fifteen steps to go. I bit my lips so that my father would not hear my teeth chattering. Ten more steps. Eight. Seven. We were walking slowly, as one follows a hearse, our own funeral procession. Only four more steps. Three. There it was now, very close to us, the pit and its flames. I gathered all that remained of my strength in order to break rank and throw myself onto the barbed wire. Deep down, I was saying good-bye to my father, to the whole universe, and, against my will, I found myself whispering the words: "*Yisgadal, veyiskadash, shmey raba* . . . May His name be exalted and sanctified . . ." My heart was about to burst. There. I was face-to-face with the Angel of Death . . .

No. Two steps from the pit, we were ordered to turn left and herded into barracks.

I squeezed my father's hand. He said:

"Do you remember Mrs. Schächter, in the train?"

NEVER SHALL I FORGET that night, the first night in camp, that turned my life into one long night seven times sealed.

Never shall I forget that smoke.

Never shall I forget the small faces of the children whose bodies I saw transformed into smoke under a silent sky.

Never shall *I* forget those flames that consumed my faith forever.

Never shall I forget the nocturnal silence that deprived me for all eternity of the desire to live.

Never shall I forget those moments that murdered my God and my soul and turned my dreams to ashes.

Never shall I forget those things, even were I condemned to live as long as God Himself.

Never.

Critical Thinking Questions

1. When he arrives at Auschwitz, Wiesel describes scenes that he "shall never forget." What scenes or experiences from the memoir do you find unforgettable?

2. At one point, after their arrival, some younger Jews consider revolting against their Nazi captors. Why do you think there were not more attempts to resist among the Jews?

3. Why must Elie lie to the SS officers and Dr. Mengele about his age and occupation?

4. How do the "veteran" prisoners respond when they discover the newcomers have never heard of Auschwitz? Why do you think Jews were not more aware of the Holocaust?

5. What effect does his experience thus far at Auschwitz appear to have on Elie's religion and belief in God?

IV. The Post-War World, 1945–Present

The Cold War

Winston Churchill's "Iron Curtain" Speech (1946)

Containment (1946)

Winston Churchill's "Iron Curtain" Speech
(1946)

On March 5, 1946, Winston Churchill, Britain's wartime prime minister, spoke about the aftermath of World War II at Westminster College in Fulton, Missouri. In the following extracts, he discusses the emergence in Europe of an "iron curtain" dividing Eastern European states liberated by the Soviets from the rest of the continent.

The United States stands at this time at the pinnacle of world power. It is a solemn moment for the American Democracy. For with primacy in power is also joined an awe-inspiring accountability to the future. If you look around you, you must feel not only the sense of duty done but also you must feel anxiety lest you fall below the level of achievement. Opportunity is here now, clear and shining for both our countries. To reject it or ignore it or fritter it away will bring upon us all the long reproaches of the after-time. It is necessary that constancy of mind, persistency of purpose, and the grand simplicity of decision shall guide and rule the conduct of the English-speaking peoples in peace as they did in war. We must, and I believe we shall, prove ourselves equal to this severe requirement.

[...]

A shadow has fallen upon the scenes so lately lighted by the Allied victory. Nobody knows what Soviet Russia and its Communist international organization intends to do in the immediate future, or what are the limits, if any, to their expansive and proselytizing tendencies. I have a strong admiration and regard for the valiant Russian people and for my wartime comrade, Marshal Stalin. There is deep sympathy and goodwill in Britain—and I doubt not here also towards the peoples of all the Russians and a resolve to persevere through many differences and rebuffs in establishing lasting friendships. We understand the Russian need to be secure on her western frontiers by the removal of all possibility of German aggression. We welcome Russia to her rightful place among the leading nations of the world. We welcome her flag upon the seas. Above all, we welcome constant, frequent and growing contacts between the Russian people and our own people on both sides of the Atlantic. It is my duty however, for I am sure you would wish me to state the facts as I see them to you, to place before you certain facts about the present position in Europe.

From Stettin in the Baltic to Trieste in the Adriatic, an iron curtain has descended across the Continent. Behind that line lie all the capitals of the ancient states of Central and Eastern Europe. Warsaw, Berlin, Prague, Vienna, Budapest, Belgrade, Bucharest and Sofia, all these famous cities and the populations around them lie in what I must call the Soviet sphere, and all are subject in one form or another, not only to Soviet influence but to a very high and, in many cases, increasing measure of control from Moscow. Athens alone—Greece with its immortal glories—is free to decide its future at an election

Reproduced with permission of Curtis Brown Ltd, London on behalf of The Estate of Winston Churchill. Copyright Winston S. Churchill.

under British, American and French observation. The Russian-dominated Polish Government has been encouraged to make enormous and wrongful inroads upon Germany, and mass expulsions of millions of Germans on a scale grievous and undreamed-of are now taking place. The Communist parties, which were very small in all these Eastern States of Europe, have been raised to preeminence and power far beyond their numbers and are seeking everywhere to obtain totalitarian control. Police governments are prevailing in nearly every case, and so far, except in Czechoslovakia, there is no true democracy.

The safety of the world requires a new unity in Europe, from which no nation should be permanently outcast. It is from the quarrels of the strong parent races in Europe that the world wars we have witnessed, or which occurred in former times, have sprung. Twice in our own lifetime we have seen the United States, against their wishes and their traditions, against arguments, the force of which it is impossible not to comprehend, drawn by irresistible forces alto these wars in time to secure the victory of the good cause, but only after frightful slaughter and devastation had occurred. Twice the United States has had to send several millions of its young men across the Atlantic to find the war; but now war can find any nation, wherever it may dwell between dusk and dawn. Surely we should work with conscious purpose for a grand pacification of Europe, within the structure of the United Nations and in accordance with its Charter. That I feel is an open cause of policy of very great importance.

In front of the iron curtain which lies across Europe are other causes for anxiety. In Italy the Communist Party is seriously hampered by having to support the Communist-trained Marshal Tito's claims to former Italian territory at the head of the Adriatic. Nevertheless the future of Italy hangs in the balance. Again one cannot imagine a regenerated Europe without a strong France. All my public life I have worked for a strong France and I never lost faith in her destiny, even in the darkest hours. I will not lose faith now. However, in a great number of countries, far from the Russian frontiers and throughout the world, Communist fifth columns are established and work in complete unity and absolute obedience to the directions they receive from the communist center. Except in the British Commonwealth and in the United States where Communism is in its infancy, the Communist parties or fifth columns constitute a growing challenge and peril to Christian civilization. These are somber facts for anyone to have to recite on the morrow of a victory gained by so much splendid comradeship in arms and in the cause of freedom and democracy; but we should be most unwise not to face them squarely while time remains.

I have felt bound to portray the shadow which, alike in the west and in the east, falls upon the world. I was a high minister at the time of the Versailles Treaty and a close friend of Mr. Lloyd-George, who was the head of the British delegation at Versailles. I did not myself agree with many things that were done, but I have a very strong impression in my mind of that situation, and I find it painful to contrast it with that which prevails now. In those days there were high hopes and unbounded confidence that the wars were over, and that the League of Nations would become all-powerful. I do not see or feel that same confidence or even the same hopes in the haggard world at the present time.

On the other hand I repulse the idea that a new war is inevitable; still more that it is imminent. It is because I am sure that our fortunes are still in our own hands and that we hold the power to save the future, that I feel the duty to speak out now that I have the occasion and the opportunity to do so. I do not believe that Soviet Russia desires war. What they desire is the fruits of war and the indefinite expansion of their power and doctrines. But what we have to consider here today while time remains, is the permanent prevention of war and the establishment of conditions of freedom and democracy as rapidly as possible in all countries. Our difficulties and dangers will not be removed by closing our eyes to them. They will not be removed by mere waiting to see what happens; nor will they be removed by a policy of appeasement. What is needed is a settlement, and the longer this is delayed, the more difficult it will be and the greater our dangers will become.

From what I have seen of our Russian friends and Allies during the war, I am convinced that there is nothing they admire so much as strength, and there is nothing for which they have less respect than for weakness, especially military weakness. For that reason the old doctrine of a balance of power is unsound. We cannot afford, if we can help it, to work on narrow margins, offering temptations to a trial of strength. If the Western Democracies stand together in strict adherence to the principles of the United Nations Charter, their influence for furthering those principles will be immense and no one is likely to molest them. If however they become divided or falter in their duty and if these all-important years are allowed to slip away, then indeed catastrophe may overwhelm us all.

Last time I saw it all coming and cried aloud to my own fellow-countrymen and to the world, but no one paid any attention. Up till the year 1933 or even 1935, Germany might have been saved from the awful fate which has overtaken her and we might all have been spared the miseries Hitler let loose upon mankind. There never was a war in all history easier to prevent by timely action than the one which has just desolated such great areas of the globe. It could have been prevented in my belief without the firing of a single shot, and Germany might be powerful, prosperous and honored today; but no one would listen and one by one we were all sucked into the awful whirlpool. We surely must not let that happen again. This can only be achieved by reaching now, in 1946, a good understanding on all points with Russia under the general authority of the United Nations Organization and by the maintenance of that good understanding through many peaceful years, by the world instrument, supported by the whole strength of the English-speaking world and all its connections. There is the solution which I respectfully offer to you in this Address to which I have given the title "The Sinews of Peace."

Critical Thinking Questions

1. How does Churchill view Russia?

2. What threats to world security does Churchill say exist beyond the "iron curtain"?

3. How does he propose that Soviet aggression should be met? What does Churchill see as the best hope for peace in Europe in the future?

Containment
(1946)

The following reading is from the "long telegram" sent in February 1946 by George F. Kennan—an official at the American Embassy in Moscow and student of Soviet affairs—to the U.S. State Department. It offers an interpretation of the potential threat to the United States presented by Soviet expansion and suggests a policy of "containment" as the appropriate U.S. response.

At bottom of Kremlin's neurotic view of world affairs is traditional and instinctive Russian sense of insecurity. Originally, this was insecurity of a peaceful agricultural people trying to live on vast exposed plain in neighborhood of fierce nomadic peoples. To this was added, as Russia came into contact with economically advanced West, fear of more competent, more powerful, more highly organized societies in that area. But this latter type of insecurity was one which afflicted rather Russian rulers than Russian people; for Russian rulers have invariably sensed that their rule was relatively archaic in form, fragile and artificial in its psychological foundation, unable to stand comparison on contact with political system of Western countries. For this reason they have always feared foreign penetration, feared direct contact between Western world and their own, feared what would happen if Russians learned truth about world without or if foreigners learned truth about world within. And they have learned to seek security only in patient but deadly struggle for total destruction of rival power, never in compacts and compromises with it.

It was no coincidence that Marxism, which had smouldered ineffectively for half a century in Western Europe, caught hold and blazed for first time in Russia. Only in this land which had never known a friendly neighbor or indeed any tolerant equilibrium of separate powers, either internal or international, could a doctrine thrive which viewed economic conflicts of society as insoluble by peaceful means. After establishment of Bolshevist regime, Marxist dogma, rendered even more truculent and intolerant by Lenin's interpretation, became a perfect vehicle for sense of insecurity with which Bolsheviks, even more than previous Russian rulers, were afflicted. In this dogma, with its basic altruism of purpose, they found justification for their instinctive fear of outside world, for the dictatorship without which they did not know how to rule, for cruelties they did not dare not to inflict, for sacrifices they felt bound to demand.... This thesis provides justification for that increase of military and police power of Russian state, for that isolation of Russian population from outside world, and for that fluid and constant pressure to extend limits of Russian police power which are together the natural and instinctive urges of Russian rulers. Basically this is only the steady advance of uneasy Russian nationalism, a centuries old movement in which conceptions of offense and defense are inextricably confused. But in new guise of international Marxism, with its honeyed promises to a desperate and war torn outside world, it is more dangerous and insidious than ever before...

Department of State, Foreign Relations of the United States, Volume 6.

On official plane we must look for following:

(a) Internal policy devoted to increasing in every way strength and prestige of Soviet state: intensive military-industrialization; maximum development of armed forces; great displays to impress outsiders; continued secretiveness about internal matters, designed to conceal weaknesses and to keep opponents in dark.

(b) Wherever it is considered timely and promising efforts will be made to advance official limits of Soviet power. For the moment, these efforts are restricted to certain neighboring points conceived of here as being of immediate strategic necessity, such as Northern Iran, Turkey, possibly Bornholm. However, other points may at any time come into question, if and as concealed Soviet political power is extended to new areas....

(c) Russians will participate officially in international organizations where they see opportunity of extending Soviet power or of inhibiting or diluting power of others. Moscow sees in UNO not the mechanism for a permanent and stable world society founded on mutual interest and aims of all nations, but an arena in which aims just mentioned can be favorably pursued....

(d) Toward colonial areas and backward or dependent peoples, Soviet policy, even on official plane, will be directed toward weakening of power and influence and contacts of advanced Western nations, on theory that in so far as this policy is successful, there will be created a vacuum which will favor Communist-Soviet penetration. Soviet pressure for participation in trusteeship arrangements thus represents, in my opinion, a desire to be in a position to complicate and inhibit exertion of Western influence at such points rather than to provide major channel for exerting of Soviet power....

(e) Russians will strive energetically to develop Soviet representation in, and official ties with, countries in which they sense strong possibilities of opposition to Western centers of power. This applies to such widely separated points as Germany, Argentina, Middle Eastern countries, etc.

(f) In international economic matters, Soviet policy will really be dominated by pursuit of autarchy for Soviet Union and Soviet-dominated adjacent areas taken together.... Soviet foreign trade may be restricted largely to Soviet's own security sphere, including occupied areas in Germany, and that a cold official shoulder may be turned to principle of general economic collaboration among nations.

(g) With respect to cultural collaboration, lip service will likewise be rendered to desirability of deepening cultural contacts between peoples, but this will not in practice be interpreted in any way which could weaken security position of Soviet peoples....

(h) Beyond this, Soviet official relations will take what might be called "correct" course with individual foreign governments, with great stress being laid on prestige of Soviet Union and its representatives and with punctilious attention to protocol, as distinct from good manners....

In summary, we have here a political force committed fanatically to the belief that with US there can be no permanent modus vivendi, that it is desirable and necessary that the internal harmony of our society be disrupted, our traditional way of life be destroyed, the international authority of our state be broken, if Soviet power is to be secure. This political force has complete power of disposition over energies of one of world's greatest people and resources of world's richest national territory, and is borne along by deep and powerful currents of Russian nationalism. In addition, it has an elaborate and far flung apparatus for exertion of its influence in other countries, an apparatus of amazing flexibility and versatility, managed by people whose experience and skill in underground methods are presumably without parallel in history. Finally, it is seemingly inaccessible to considerations of reality in its basic reactions. For it, the vast fund of objective fact about human society is not, as with us, the measure against which outlook is constantly being tested and reformed, but a grab bag from which individual items are selected arbitrarily and tendentiously to bolster an outlook already preconceived. This is admittedly not a pleasant picture. Problem of how to cope with this force [is] undoubtedly greatest task our diplomacy has ever faced and probably greatest it will ever have to face. It should be point of departure from which our political general staff work at present juncture should proceed. It should be approached with same thoroughness and care as solution of major strategic problem in war and if necessary, with no smaller outlay in planning effort. I cannot attempt to suggest all answers here. But I would like to record my conviction there are certain observations of a more encouraging nature I should like to make:

1. Soviet power, unlike that of Hitlerite Germany, is neither schematic nor adventuristic. It does not work by fixed plans. It does not take unnecessary risks. Impervious to logic of reason, and it is highly sensitive to logic of force. For this reason it can easily withdraw—and usually does—when strong resistance is encountered at any point. Thus, if the adversary has sufficient force and makes clear his readiness to use it, he rarely has to do so. If situations are properly handled there need be no prestige-engaging showdowns.
2. Gauged against Western World as a whole, Soviets are still by far the weaker force. Thus, their success will really depend on degree of cohesion, firmness and vigor which Western World can muster. And this is factor which it is within our power to influence.
3. Success of Soviet system, as form of internal power, is not yet finally proven. It has yet to be demonstrated that it can survive supreme test of successive transfer of power from one individual or group to another.... In Russia, party has now become a great and—for the moment—highly successful apparatus of dictatorial administration, but it has ceased to be a source of emotional inspiration. Thus, internal soundness and permanence of movement need not yet be regarded as assured.
4. All Soviet propaganda beyond Soviet security sphere is basically negative and destructive. It should therefore be relatively easy to combat it by any intelligent and really constructive program. For these reasons I think we may approach calmly and with good heart problem of how to deal with Russia. As to how this approach should be made, I only wish to advance, by way of conclusion, following comments:

(1) Our first step must be to apprehend, and recognize for what it is, the nature of the movement with which we are dealing. We must study it with same courage, detachment, objectivity, and same determination not to be emotionally provoked or unseated by it, with which doctor studies unruly and unreasonable individual.

(2) We must see that our public is educated to realities of Russian situation. I cannot over-emphasize importance of this. Press cannot do this alone. It must be done mainly by Government, which is necessarily more experienced and better informed on practical problems involved....

(3) Much depends on health and vigor of our own society. World communism is like malignant parasite which feeds only on diseased tissue. This is point at which domestic and foreign policies meet. Every courageous and incisive measure to solve internal problems of our own society to improve self-confidence, discipline, morale, and community spirit of our own people, is a diplomatic victory over Moscow worth a thousand diplomatic notes and joint communiques....

(4) We must formulate and put forward for other nations a much more positive and constructive picture of sort of world we would like to see than we have put forward in past. It is not enough to urge people to develop political processes similar to our own. Many foreign peoples, in Europe at least, are tired and frightened by experiences of past, and are less interested in abstract freedom than in security. They are seeking guidance rather than responsibilities. We should be better able than Russians to give them this. And unless we do, Russians certainly will.

(5) Finally we must have courage and self-confidence to cling to our own methods and conceptions of human society. After all, the greatest danger that can befall us in coping with this problem of Soviet communism, is that we shall allow ourselves to become like those with whom we are coping.

Critical Thinking Questions

1. What qualities of the Russian character, history, or culture does Kennan think have made it well suited to Marxism?

2. What is the goal of the Soviet Union? What steps does Kennan warn it will take in pursuit of this goal?

3. In dealing with the Soviet Union, what advantages does Kennan feel the West (or the United States) has?

Decolonization and Its Aftermath in the Non-Western World

Gandhi on the Spinning Wheel and Satyagraha

Vietnamese Declaration of Independence (1945)

UN Declaration on Decolonization (1962)

Julius Nyerere on One-Party Rule in Tanganyika (1961)

José A. Silva Michelena, The Illusion of Democracy in Dependent Nations *(1971)*

Genocide in Rwanda (1994)

Osama bin Laden, "Hypocrisy Rears Its Ugly Head" (2001)

Gandhi on the Spinning Wheel and Satyagraha

For more than three decades, Mohandas Karamchand Gandhi (1869–1948) led India's struggle for independence from Britain. His efforts were rewarded in 1947 when the British finally pulled out. Throughout his political life, Gandhi advocated peaceful methods of resistance, stressed the importance of tradition over innovation, and urged unity among all Indians. Sadly, Gandhi was assassinated in 1948.

On Truth

My uniform experience has convinced me that there is no other God than Truth. . . . The only means for the realization of Truth is *Ahimsa*. . . . After all, however sincere my strivings after *Ahimsa* may have been, they have still been imperfect and inadequate. The little fleeting glimpses, therefore, that I have been able to have of Truth can hardly convey an idea of the indescribable lustre of Truth, a million times more intense than that of the sun we daily see with our eyes. In fact what I have caught is only the faintest glimmer of that mighty effulgence. But this much I can say with assurance, as a result of all my experiments, that a perfect vision of Truth can only follow a complete realization of *Ahimsa*.

To see the universal and all-pervading Spirit of Truth face to face one must be able to love the meanest of creation as oneself. And a man who aspires after that cannot afford to keep out of any field of life. That is why my devotion to Truth has drawn me into the field of politics; and I can say without the slightest hesitation, and yet in all humility, that those who say that religion has nothing to do with politics do not know what religion means.

Identification with everything that lives is impossible without self-purification; without self-purification the observance of the law of *Ahimsa* must remain an empty dream; God can never be realized by one who is not pure of heart. Self-purification therefore must mean purification in all the walks of life. And purification being highly infectious, purification of oneself necessarily leads to the purification of one's surroundings.

But the path of self-purification is hard and steep. To attain to perfect purity one has to become absolutely passion-free in thought, speech and action; to rise above the opposing currents of love and hatred, attachment and repulsion. I know that I have not in me as yet that triple purity, in spite of constant ceaseless striving for it. That is why the world's praise fails to move me, indeed it very often stings me. To conquer the subtle passions seems to me to be harder far than the physical conquest to the world by the force of arms. Ever since my return to India I have had experiences of the dormant passions lying hidden within me. The knowledge of them has made me feel humiliated though not defeated. The experiences and experiments have sustained me and given me great joy. But I know that I have still before me a difficult path to traverse. I must reduce myself to zero. So long as a man does not of his own free will put himself last among his fellow creatures, there is no salvation for him. *Ahimsa* is the farthest limit of humility.

Copyright © Navajivan Trust. Reprinted by permission.

The Spinning Wheel

A starving man thinks first of satisfying his hunger before anything else. The celebrated incident of a disciplined sage like Vishwamitra, whose austerities have hardly been matched, stooping even to steal forbidden food when he was famishing, shows the stress under which a starving man labours. He will sell his liberty and all for the sake of getting a morsel of food. Sailors struggling for want of food in mid-ocean have been known to resort to cannibalism in order to satisfy their hunger. Such is the position of millions of the people of India. For them, liberty, God, and all such words are merely letters put together without the slightest meaning. They jar upon them. They will extend a welcome to any person who comes to them with a morsel of food. And if we want to give these people a sense of freedom we shall have to provide them with work which they can easily do in their desolate homes and which would give them at least the barest living. This can only be done by the spinning-wheel. And when they have become self-reliant and are able to support themselves, we are in a position to talk to them about freedom, about Congress, etc. Those therefore who bring them work and means of getting a crust of bread will be their deliverers and will be also the people who will make them hunger for liberty. Hence the political value of the spinning-wheel, apart from its further ability to displace foreign cloth and thus remove the greatest temptation in the way of Englishmen to hold India.

Satyagraha, Civil Disobedience, Passive Resistance, Non-co-operation

It is often my lot to answer knotty questions on all sorts of topics arising out of this great movement of national purification. A company of collegiate non-co-operators asked me to define for them the terms which I have used as heading for this note. And even at this late day, I was seriously asked whether *satyagraha* did not at times warrant resistance by violence, as for instance in the case of a sister whose virtue might be in danger from a desperado. I ventured to suggest that it was the completest defence without irritation, without being ruffled, to interpose oneself between the victim and the victimizer, and to face death. I added that this (for the assailant) novel method of defence would, in all probability, exhaust his passion and he would no longer want to ravish an innocent woman, but would want to flee from her presence for very shame, and that, if he did not, the act of personal bravery on the part of her brother would steel her heart for putting up an equally brave defence and resisting the lust of a man turned brute for the while. And I thought I clinched my argument by saying that if, in spite of all the defence, the unexpected happened, and the physical force of the tyrant overpowered his victim, the disgrace would not be that of the woman but of her assailant and that both she and her brother, who died in the attempt to defend her virtue, would stand well before the Throne of Judgment. I do not warrant that my argument convinced my listener or that it would convince the reader. The world I know will go on as before. But it is well at this moment of self-examination to understand and appreciate the implications of the powerful movement of non-violence. All religions have emphasized the highest ideal but all have more or less permitted departures as so many concessions to human weaknesses.

I now proceed to summarize the explanations I gave of the various terms. It is beyond my capacity to give accurate and terse definitions.

Satyagraha, then, is literally holding on to Truth and it means, therefore, Truth-force. Truth is soul or spirit. It is, therefore, known as soul-force. It excludes the use of violence because man is not capable of knowing the absolute truth and, therefore, not competent to punish. The word was coined in South Africa to distinguish the non-violent resistance of the Indians of South Africa from the contemporary 'passive resistance' of the suffragettes and others. It is not conceived as a weapon of the weak.

Passive resistance is used in the orthodox English sense and covers the suffragette movement as well as the resistance of the nonconformists. Passive resistance has been conceived and is regarded as a weapon of the weak. Whilst it avoids violence, being not open to the weak, it does not exclude its use if, in the opinion of a passive resister, the occasion demands it. However, it has always been distinguished from armed resistance and its application was at one time confined to Christian martyrs.

Civil disobedience is civil breach of unmoral statutory enactments. The expression was, so far as I am aware, coined by Thoreau to signify his own resistance to the laws of a slave state.

Critical Thinking Questions

1. What must a person do to realize Truth? How is it achieved?

2. In the section entitled "The Spinning Wheel," what basic problem does Gandhi identify? How does he think the spinning wheel can help address this problem?

3. From the section on *satyagraha,* what does Gandhi appear to believe is the ultimate reason why *satyagraha* and passive resistance are the most appropriate methods of resistance for India to adopt in its struggle for independence?

Vietnamese Declaration of Independence
(1945)

Vietnam was a French colony prior to World War II and a Japanese colony during the war. After the Japanese had been chased out in 1945, France attempted to reassert control. The Vietnamese Communist Party led by Ho Chi Minh, however, was determined that Vietnam should become an independent republic, to which end the following document was written. The West, however, ignored the declaration and supported French claims, laying the basis not only for a protracted French-Vietnamese struggle but also for the subsequent Vietnam War.

"All men are created equal. They are endowed by their Creator with certain inalienable rights; among these are Life, Liberty, and the pursuit of Happiness."

This immortal statement was made in the Declaration of Independence of the United States of America in *1776*. In a broader sense, this means: All the peoples on the earth are equal from birth, all the peoples have a right to live, to be happy and free.

The Declaration of the French Revolution made in *1791* on the Rights of Man and the Citizen also states: "All men are born free and with equal rights, and must always remain free and have equal rights."

Those are undeniable truths.

Nevertheless, for more than eighty years, the French imperialists, abusing the standard of Liberty, Equality, and Fraternity, have violated our Fatherland and oppressed our fellowcitizens. They have acted contrary to the ideals of humanity and justice.

In the field of politics, they have deprived our people of every democratic liberty.

They have enforced inhuman laws; they have set up three distinct political regimes in the North, the Center, and the South of Vietnam in order to wreck our national unity and prevent our people from being united.

They have built more prisons than schools. They have mercilessly slain our patriots; they have drowned our uprisings in rivers of blood.

They have fettered public opinion; they have practised obscurantism against our people.

To weaken our race they have forced us to use opium and alcohol.

In the field of economics, they have fleeced us to the backbone, impoverished our people, and devastated our land.

They have robbed us of our rice fields, our mines, our forests, and our raw materials. They have monopolized the issuing of banknotes and the export trade.

They have invented numerous unjustifiable taxes and reduced our people, especially our peasantry, to a state of extreme poverty.

They have hampered the prospering of our national bourgeoisie; they have mercilessly exploited our workers.

In the autumn of 1940, when the Japanese Fascists violated Indochina's territory to establish new bases in their fight against the Allies, the French imperialists went down on their bended knees and handed over our country to them.

From *Selected Writings*, Hanoi: Foreign Language Publishing House.

Thus, from that date, our people were subjected to the double yoke of the French and the Japanese. Their sufferings and miseries increased. The result was that from the end of last year to the beginning of this year, from Quang Tri province to the North of Vietnam, more than two million of our fellow citizens died from starvation. On March 9, the French troops were disarmed by the Japanese. The French colonialists either fled or surrendered showing that not only were they incapable of "protecting" us, but that, in the span of five years, they had twice sold our country to the Japanese.

On several occasions before March 9, the Vietminh League urged the French to ally themselves with it against the Japanese. Instead of agreeing to this proposal, the French colonialists so intensified their terrorist activities against the Vietminh members that before fleeing they massacred a great number of our political prisoners detained at Yen Bay and Caobang.

Notwithstanding all this, our fellow citizens have always manifested toward the French a tolerant and humane attitude. Even after the Japanese putsch of March 1945, the Vietminh League helped many Frenchmen to cross the frontier, rescued some of them from Japanese jails, and protected French lives and property.

From the autumn of 1940, our country had in fact ceased to be a French colony and had become a Japanese possession.

After the Japanese had surrendered to the Allies, our whole people rose to regain our national sovereignty and to found the Democratic Republic of Vietnam.

The truth is that we have wrested our independence from the Japanese and not from the French.

The French have fled, the Japanese have capitulated, Emperor Bao Dai has abdicated. Our people have broken the chains which for nearly a century have fettered them and have won independence for the Fatherland. Our people at the same time have overthrown the monarchic regime that has reigned supreme for dozens of centuries. In its place has been established the present Democratic Republic.

For these reasons, we, members of the Provisional Government, representing the whole Vietnamese people, declare that from now on we break off all relations of a colonial character with France; we repeal all the international obligation that France has so far subscribed to on behalf of Vietnam and we abolish all the special rights the French have unlawfully acquired in our Fatherland.

The whole Vietnamese people, animated by a common purpose, are determined to fight to the bitter end against any attempt by the French colonialists to reconquer their country.

We are convinced that the Allied nations, which at Tehran and San Francisco have acknowledged the principles of self-determination and equality of nations, will not refuse to acknowledge the independence of Vietnam.

A people who have courageously opposed French domination for more than eight years, a people who have fought side by side with the Allies against the Fascists during these last years, such a people must be free and independent.

For these reasons, we, members of the Provisional Government of the Democratic Republic of Vietnam, solemnly declare to the world that Vietnam has the right to be a free and independent country—and in fact is so already. The entire Vietnamese people are determined to mobilize all their physical and mental strength, to sacrifice their lives and property in order to safeguard their independence and liberty.

Critical Thinking Questions

1. Why do you think the document begins by quoting Thomas Jefferson's Declaration of Independence and the French Declaration of the Rights of Man and of the Citizen?

2. According to the document, what has been the impact of colonialism on the Vietnamese people, their government, and society?

3. What do you think is the single most effective claim made in the document in behalf of Vietnamese independence? Justify your answer.

UN Declaration on Decolonization
(1962)

Created in the wake of World War II to work for global security, the United Nations quickly came to see decolonization as an area in which it both could and should play a critical role, as the following declaration makes clear.

The General Assembly: . . .

Recognizing that the peoples of the world ardently desire the end of colonialism in all its manifestations, . . .

Convinced that the continued existence of colonialism prevents the development of international economic co-operation, impedes the social, cultural and economic development of dependent peoples and militates against the United Nations ideal of universal peace,

Believing that the process of liberation is irresistible and that, in order to avoid serious crises, an end must be put to colonialism, and all practices of segregation and discrimination associated therewith, . . .

Convinced that all peoples have an inalienable right to complete freedom, the exercise of their sovereignty and the integrity of their national territory,

Solemnly proclaims the necessity of bringing to a speedy and unconditional end colonialism in all its forms and manifestations:

And to this end DECLARES THAT:

1. The subjection of peoples to alien subjugation, domination and exploitation constitutes a denial of fundamental rights, is contrary to the Charter of the United Nations and is an impediment to the promotion of world peace and co-operation. . . .

3. Inadequacy of political, economic, social or educational preparation should never serve as a pretext for delaying independence.

4. All armed action or repressive measures of all kinds directed against dependent peoples shall cease in order to enable them to exercise peacefully and freely their right to complete independence. . . .

5. Immediate steps shall be taken, in Trust and Non-Self-Governing Territories or all other territories which have not yet attained independence to transfer all powers to the peoples of those territories, without any conditions or reservations, in accordance with their freely expressed will and desire, without any distinction as to race, creed or colour, in order to enable them to enjoy complete independence and freedom.

From Report of the Special Committee on the Situation with Regard to the Implementation of the Declaration on the Granting of Independence to Colonial Countries and Peoples.

Critical Thinking Questions

1. Based on the document, could the UN be regarded as "on the side of" either the colonizers or the colonized? Justify your answer.

2. Rewrite article 3 in your own words. What criticisms might it be possible to make of this article? What arguments could be made in its favor?

Julius Nyerere on One-Party Rule in Tanganyika
(1961)

In 1961, immediately prior to Tanganyika's independence, its prime minister, Julius Nyerere, outlined what he felt was the appropriate form democracy should take in Africa.

The African concept of democracy is similar to that of the ancient Greeks from whose language the word "democracy" originated. To the Greeks, democracy meant simply "government by discussion among equals." The people discussed and when they reached agreement the result was a "people's decision."

Mr. Guy Clutton-Brock, writing about Nyasaland, describes traditional African democracy as: "The elders sit under the big tree and talk until they agree." This "talking until you agree" is the essential of the traditional African concept of democracy.

To minds molded by western parliamentary traditions and western concepts of democratic institutions, the idea of an organized opposition group has become so familiar that its absence immediately raises the cry of "dictatorship." It is no good telling them that when a group of 100 equals have sat and talked together until they agreed to dig a well (and "until they agreed" implies that they will have produced many conflicting arguments before they did eventually agree), they have practiced democracy. Proponents of western parliamentary traditions will consider whether the opposition was organized and therefore automatic, or whether it was spontaneous and therefore free. Only if it was automatic will they concede that here was democracy.

Basically, democracy is government by discussion as opposed to government by force, and by discussion between the people or their chosen representatives as opposed to a hereditary clique. Under the tribal system, whether there was a chief or not, African society was a society of equals and it conducted its business by discussion.

It is true that this "pure" democracy—the totally unorganized "talking until you agree"—can no longer be adequate; it is too clumsy a way of conducting the affairs of a large modern State. But the need to organize the "government by discussion" does not necessarily imply the need to organize an opposition group as part of the system.

I am not arguing that the two-party system is not democratic, I am only saying that it is simply one form which democracy happens to have taken in certain countries and that it is by no means essential. I am sure that even my friends in the Labour Party or the Conservative Party in Britain would admit that if their party could succeed in winning all the seats, they would be perfectly happy to form a one-party government. They—the winning party, that is—would not be likely to suspect themselves of having suddenly turned Britain into a dictatorship!

Some of us have been over-ready to swallow unquestioningly the proposition that you cannot have democracy unless you have a second party to oppose the party in power. But, however difficult our

---

From *Spearhead* by Julius Nyerere. Reproduced in Atlas, Volume III, March 1962.

friends in Britain and America may find it to accept what to them is a new idea—that democracy can exist where there is no formal opposition—I think we in Africa should think very carefully before we abandon our traditional attitude.

It is often overlooked that the Anglo-Saxon tradition of a two-party system is a reflection of the society in which it evolved. Within that society there was a struggle between the "haves" and the "have-nots"—each of whom organized themselves into political parties, one party associated with wealth and the status quo and the other with the masses of the people and change. Thus the existence of distinct classes in a society and the struggle between them resulted in the growth of the two-party system. But need this be accepted as the essential and only pattern of democracy?

With rare exceptions the idea of class is something entirely foreign to Africa. Here in this continent the nationalist movements are fighting a battle for freedom from foreign domination, not from domination by any ruling class of our own. To us "the other party" is the colonial power. In many parts of Africa this struggle has been won; in others it is still going on. But everywhere the people who fight the battle are not former overlords wanting to re-establish a lost authority; they are not a rich mercantile class whose freedom to exploit the masses is limited by the colonial powers; they are the common people of Africa.

Thus once the foreign power—"the other party"—has been expelled there is no ready-made division, and it is by no means certain that democracy will adopt the same machinery and symbols as the Anglo-Saxon. Nor indeed is it necessarily desirable that it should.

New nations like Tanganyika are merging into independence as a result of a struggle for freedom which leaves no room for differences and which unites all elements in the country; and the nationalists movements—having united the people and led them to freedom—must inevitably form the first government of the new states. Once the first free government is formed, its supreme task lies ahead—the building up of the country's economy so as to raise the living standards of the people, the eradication of disease and the banishment of ignorance and superstition. This, no less than the struggle against colonialism, calls for the maximum united effort by the whole country if it is to succeed. *There can be no room for difference or division.*

In western democracies it is an accepted practice in times of emergency for opposition parties to sink their differences and join together in forming a national government. *This is our time of emergency;* and until our war against poverty, ignorance and disease has been won we should not let our unity be destroyed by a desire to follow somebody else's "book of rules."...

In the past all that was required of government was merely to maintain law and order within the country and to protect it from external aggression. Today the responsibilities of governments, whether "Communist" or "free," are infinitely wide. However nearly its requirements of money and men may be met, no government today finds it easy to fulfill all its responsibilities to the people.

To the demands of the common man in Africa, intensified as they are by the vivid contrast between his own lot and that of others in more developed countries, add the lack of means at the disposal of the African governments to meet these demands: the lack of men, the lack of money, above all the lack of time. To all this add the very nature of the new countries themselves. They are usually countries without natural unity. Their "boundaries" enclose those artificial units carved out of Africa by grabbing colonial powers without any consideration for ethnic groups or geographical realities, so that these countries now include within their borders tribal groups which, until the coming of the European powers, had never been under one government. To these, in the case of East and Central Africa, you must add the new tribes from Asia, the Middle East, and Europe. Here are divisions enough to pose a truly formidable task in nation-building.

It should be obvious, then, why the governments of these new countries must treat the situation as one of national emergency, comparable to that of a country at war. In the early days of nation-building as in time of war the opposition, if any, must act even more responsibly than an opposition in a more developed and more stable, a more unified and better-equipped country in times of peace. Given such a responsible opposition, I would be the first person to defend its rights. But where is it? Too often the only voices to be heard in "opposition" are those of a few irresponsible individuals who exploit the very privileges of democracy—freedom of the press, freedom of association, freedom to criticize in order to deflect the government from its responsibilities to the people by creating problems of law and order.

The admitted function of any political opposition is to try and persuade the electorate to reject the existing government at the next election. This is reasonable in the case of a responsible opposition with a definite alternative policy in which its members sincerely believe; but that sort of mature opposition is rare indeed in a newly independent state. Usually the irresponsible individuals I have mentioned have neither sincerity, conviction nor any policy at all save that of self-aggrandizement. They merely employ the catch phrases copied from the political language of older, stable countries, in order to engage the sympathy of the unthinking for their destructive tactics. Nor are the tactics they use those of a responsible democratic opposition. In such circumstances the government must deal firmly and promptly with the troublemakers. The country cannot afford, during these vital early years of its life, to treat such people with the same degree of tolerance which may be safely allowed in a long-established democracy.

To those who wonder if democracy can survive in Africa my own answer, then, would be that, far from its being an alien idea, democracy has long been familiar to the African. There is nothing in our traditional attitude to discussion, and current dedication to human rights, to justify the claim that democracy is in danger in Africa. I see exactly the opposite: the principles of our nationalist struggles for human dignity, augmented by our traditional attitude to discussion, should augur well for democracy in Africa.

Critical Thinking Questions

1. According to Nyerere, how do Africans define democracy? How does the traditional African concept of democracy differ from that of Western democracies?

2. According to Nyerere, what is it about African history or circumstances that makes a different approach to democracy appropriate?

3. Specifically, what obstacles do African leaders face in their attempts to build unified, independent nations?

4. What steps does Nyerere believe African governments should take to overcome these obstacles to nation building?

José A. Silva Michelena, The Illusion of Democracy in Dependent Nations

(1971)

Silva Michelena, a Venezuelan scholar, here argues that Latin American nations, including his own, have developed historically and remain today in a position of economic dependency on other powers—the Spanish and Portuguese in earlier times and the United States today. Such a situation, he argues, continues to limit the potential for economic growth and political independence in Latin American nations.

The general law that describes underdevelopment as a process has been briefly expressed as follows:

> Capitalism inserts, in a precapitalist structure, a foreign sector which gives origin to and fosters a deformed and dependent capitalist growth which generates the conditions for its own stagnation or involution.[1]

In order to understand this definition we must review history, though concisely, in order to lay bare the roots of the process. If we know how deep the roots lie, we shall better understand the enormous effort that must go into the uprooting.

What is today called Latin America was discovered when the European capitalist nations were expanding throughout the world in search of new trade routes, new markets, and primary resources. At that time, Spain and Portugal had some industry and carried on minor trade with other European countries, but they were in no sense dynamic centers of capitalism. They were, in fact, quite independent of the European centers of mercantilism. For this reason, the impact of their colonization policies was different from that of the countries which were to control the industrial revolution in Europe.

England and France, for example, permitted sizable emigration to their colonies not only to ensure supplies of raw materials but also to enlarge export markets. These markets could be maintained and broadened only if colonists to the new world were permitted reasonable latitude in the development of the lands they had occupied. Their purchasing power, obviously, depended on their own economic growth.

The economies of the Portuguese-Spanish colonies were organized on a different and extremely rigid pattern. The colonies were viewed by the mother countries as sources of wealth (gold) and raw materials, not as potential markets. Colonial policies were therefore tailored to ensure that the colonies would develop no national sense of their own. The forms of guaranteeing dependency were various. Both Spain and Portugal established intermediary centers (for example, Buenos Aires and Mexico City) between the colonies and the metropolis (the imperial states). This system guaranteed to Spain

---

From *The Illusion of Democracy in Dependent Nations* by Jose A. Silva Michelena. Reprinted by permission of MIT Press.

and Portugal both their monopoly of commerce and an effective control over the colonies.

The Spaniards, in this drive to maintain their colonies separate from, but dependent on, predetermined power centers, granted exclusive rights to carry on commerce to Spaniards sent out from the mother country. This policy was aimed also at maintaining the largest margin of profits possible for Spain. Their second major technique for averting any possible development of independent political structures in the colonies was to appoint only Spaniards in important political positions. Such arrangements effectively shut off the possibility that the criollos would be able to control their own destinies. Despite their Spanish descent and what would seem to have been their logical right to benefit from their economic activities and to control their political destiny, they were limited to agrarian activities—albeit on large plantations—and to minor political offices in the city. The situation might have been altered if there had been large-scale emigration from Spain and Portugal, but there was not. Instead, this dependent and atomized economy was firmly established, affecting not only the ecology of populated centers and the means of communications but also the distribution of products and the exercise of power.

In Venezuela, which was a poor and therefore weak link in the chain of control, the *latifundista* class—criollo owners of large plantations—prospered, principally by cultivating cacao. What other agricultural products were grown were for local consumption. From its base of the cacao plantations, which were concentrated in the central region of Venezuela, the *latifundista* class emerged with enough power to challenge the Spaniards. This class gradually began to demand more participation in the economic and political control of the region. Antagonism between what had by then become two dominant classes therefore had two mutually reinforcing sources: first, hostilities between plantation owners and merchants and, second, those between criollos and Spaniards.

The social structure as a whole was conditioned by the mode of production of the latifundia, which had organizational characteristics similar to feudal modes of production but produced for a world capitalist market. Part of the labor force was slave, but most of it was made up of "free" workers of varying degrees of indenture. Meanwhile, a middle sector developed in the cities, composed of marginal whites and pardos (racially mixed persons) who worked in minor jobs but whose aspiration was to be incorporated into the total structure.

Two significant events helped to sharpen the conflicts between the dominant classes. First, the establishment and operation of the Compañia Guipuzcoana not only centralized and controlled the national market but also fostered the institutionalization of the organs of political control and made them more rigid. Second, at the end of the eighteenth century, the collapse of the cacao market seriously affected the volume of exports. A further factor was the weakening of Spanish control due to the French occupation of Spain.

All of the events just described were among those leading to the wars of independence. With political independence came the possibility of transforming the colonies into autonomous centers, because finally the alternative of an indigenous development of capitalism was open. But this alternative was never adopted, because the criollos retained the economic and political patterns of the past.

The criollos, both during the war of independence and afterward, concentrated on keeping the economy linked with the world capitalist market through the exploitation and export of a new primary product, coffee, which was to substitute for the declining cacao.

First of all, it should be understood that Western political institutions were not created by chance. They were structured to meet the needs to administer, guide, and facilitate the development of the new capitalist relations of production and distribution being established throughout Europe. Thus, the development of industry created not only a new mode of work—"free work"—but also a new form of organizing production—a hierarchical system. This system is ultimately imposed on society through state bureaucracy. Along with the consolidation of markets, national boundaries were defined.

In Venezuela, as in most of Latin America, these stages of nationalization were not reached until the twentieth century, when an integrated national market had been established. Consequently, until recently Venezuela was not a nation in the conventional historical sense, because there had been no socioeconomic requirement for it to become one. Throughout the nineteenth century the region was basically an exporter of primary products; this condition helped to maintain the "islands" or regional centers, economically dependent on a world market but ruled by local caudillos who were constantly struggling with one another to gain central control.

At this stage, three dominant classes had developed: the *latifundistas,* the importers and their administrators, and the *latifundista* generals. Although they held considerable local control, they were still under a dependent structure, subordinate to decisions they did not control. The backwardness of the productive forces made organization of the masses almost impossible. Instead, they were used alternatively as soldiers or as semifree workers. The lowest classes, then, were subjected to both internal and external domination and profited not at all from their own work.

Toward the end of the nineteenth century a crisis in the world coffee market created a new and profound political crisis in Venezuela. The Andean region, where most of the important coffee plantations were located, suffered the most. Logically, the Andeans began a military invasion to the center. By the turn of the century they had gained national power. Meanwhile, foreign loans and investments increased, although not at the same pace as in other Latin American countries such as Argentina and Brazil. Nevertheless, the blockage of Puerto Cabello by foreign navies, as well as other international incidents, were political symptoms that the nature of dependency was changing.

Like the criollos after the wars of independence, the new Andean elite too showed no interest in changing the economic structure of the country; the entrepreneurs of those days were economically and culturally incapable of launching an industrialization program. Conditions such as this are perfect for establishing an economy of enclave. In Venezuela it was oil, which requires an accumulation of capital and a technological capacity well beyond that of the local entrepreneurs. Every Venezuelan petit bourgeois individual tried to grab a share of the enormous benefits the oil business was producing. Because of these factors the oil industry in its initial stages developed almost without national control. The companies exploiting the oil resources were able therefore to take advantage of all the facilities offered by an agrarian-based government elite and a dependent bourgeoisie that saw, in urban land speculation and financial operations, unlimited opportunities for easy profit taking at small risk.

The peculiar character of the Venezuelan economic pattern of growth stems from this history. Its special consequence was that during the economic crisis of the 1930s, when other Latin American countries were pushing industrialization forward by means of import substitution, Venezuela kept growing outward. Its economic infrastructure was built on an untransformed dependent urban economy and agrarian structure. This phase of "simple growth," as Armando Córdova and Héctor Silva Michelena call it, had as its principal motive power the export sector of the economy.

Only during World War II did a few Venezuelan entrepreneurs, spurred by the trade limitations imposed by the war, begin to establish import-substituting industries. Thus, by 1950, when the world oil market was beginning to diminish its rate of growth, both national industry and the bourgeoisie were still at the primary level of development. The decision of the military dictator Pérez Jiménez to modernize the country through a program of public works—building magnificent highways, hotels, and so forth—was simply a variation of a system of dependent economic growth. The policy not only failed to generate a national, independent bourgeoisie but further engendered a bourgeoisie linked with and subordinated to the bourgeoisie of the dominant countries, especially of the United States.

Even so, what economic growth occurred did transform the conditions of existence of many Venezuelans of the middle sector, workers, and peasants. It also created a new phenomenon, a marginal population that was gradually but swiftly occupying the most visible—and least adequate for living—sites in and around the cities. Contrary to what had happened in the advanced capitalist countries, where the growth of the cities followed the growth of industry, Venezuelan cities took form before, and faster than, industry.

These economic facts, however, only rose to the surface, and therefore to the common consciousness of Venezuelans, between 1956 and 1959, when oil exports, and consequently fiscal revenues, decreased from 9 to 4 percent per year. This crisis forced both government and business to recognize the need to industrialize the country. With the inauguration of the democratic regime that deposed Pérez Jiménez, a crash program of import substitution was begun. This euphoric phase is already approaching its end. Almost all consumer goods, which are easy to substitute, are being produced internally. The process is now beginning to enter a new and more complex phase that requires more highly developed technology and more capital.

It is still too early to predict exactly what will happen. There are signs, however, that Venezuela is following the same course that was taken by Brazil and Argentina, that is, domination of industry by foreign capital—denationalization. Yet the key question here is why the Venezuelan bourgeoisie—now supposedly stronger and more class conscious—is incapable of conducting an autonomous national process of industrialization. There are several answers to this question, but we shall deal with the two crucial ones: the first is politicoeconomic; the second, technical.

The main thesis proposed here is that, as the process of import substitution continues, Venezuelan entrepreneurs are becoming weaker and less "Venezuelan." They are less Venezuelan in the sense that, with the increasing participation of large U.S. corporations in providing both capital and technology, control of the whole process of industrialization is moving into the hands of North Americans. Venezuelan entrepreneurs are less strong, because they lack the technical capacity, entrepreneurial spirit, and nationalism essential for an autonomous leadership. These are fatal weaknesses at a time when the industrializing process is becoming ever more complex and requires ever more complex technical training.

Again using Brazil and Argentina, where the process of denationalization is more advanced, as models for prediction, what can be anticipated for Venezuela? In the first phase, Venezuelan capital will merge with North American capital, with the latter rapidly gaining control of all light industries, such as rum, tobacco, and food. In a second phase, which might even be simultaneous with the first, medium and heavy industries will be established with more or less equal participation between local government and North American capital but relying heavily on North American technology. With such arrangements, we must assume that in this phase Venezuelan entrepreneurs will remain marginal. In the final phase, it is likely that the state will sell all the industrial complex, industry by industry, to large foreign corporations. Meanwhile, the Venezuelan bourgeoisie will retain control of the financial and commercial sectors, of construction and urban development, and of agricultural enterprises and will increasingly invest its profits in the New York stock market or place them in foreign banks.

Although loss of control of the key economic sector (industry) will make the Venezuelan bourgeoisie weaker as a force for economic nationalism, it will not become less important in internal politics. On the contrary, its own direct economic interests, together with its marginal participation in the heavy industry sector, already are being accompanied by an increasing political activity and class consciousness that is leading toward more open and effective use of special-interest organizations (particularly the Federation of Chambers of Commerce and Production, FEDECAMARAS) to exercise political pressure. These organizations are no longer merely defending themselves against government arbitrariness, as was the case in the late forties and early fifties; they are now geared toward guiding government economic policy. Their political philosophy, which underlies the economic process just described, as Frank Bonilla amply documents, might be expressed in a paraphrase of the statement that once rocked U.S. politics: "What is good for Fedecamaras is good for the nation."[2]

Let us assume, for the moment, that the Venezuelan bourgeoisie is culturally and politically able to confront and undertake the second phase of import substitution, industrialization, autonomously. What would be the likelihood of its success? To date, there is little if any capacity within Venezuela to generate the technology required to establish such industrial complexes. Inevitably, then, under the present form of political organization, it would have to adopt methods of production and forms of organization and control imposed by those who own the technology. Hence, it would continue to be subordinate to foreign capitalists.

Although a number of theorists recognize the risk of adopting technology produced in advanced countries, they feel that such use also has great advantages. Brazilian economist Celso Furtado recently pointed out the fallacy in this assumption.[3] Latin American entrepreneurs (assuming they have accumulated the capital and have the cultural disposition to do so) may choose from a wide spectrum of ready-made technology, which makes it unnecessary for them to invest in creating it. But how real is this advantage in the light of the needs of society? The technology of advanced countries is developed primarily around the goals of saving both labor and raw materials—perhaps the only abundant resources in underdeveloped countries. Thus the adoption of the technology tends only to worsen unemployment structurally—in terms of the classes in which it is the greatest problem—and to diminish the overall impact of new investments on the national economy. Furthermore, almost inevitably the adoption of a foreign technology is linked to dependence on those foreign groups that produce it, leading, in the end, to the denationalization of the economy.

Adoption of alien technology, however, has further consequences for underdeveloped societies. Armando Córdova, for example, points out that foreign technology imposes alien patterns of consumption, which, in turn, brake the development of national productive forces:

> Production not only provides materials to fulfill needs; it also provides needs for materials.... The need for an object that consumers experience has been created by perception of such object.... Thus production not only produces an object for a subject but also produces a subject for an object.[4]

Interdependently and dynamically, then, both processes reinforce the dependency of the peripheral country on a technologically and economically dominant one.

Furthermore, within the dependent country, the local bases of science and technology and, in general, of the culture consequent on developments in the productive process are judged according to foreign patterns and standards. This consequence not only reinforces the use of alien technology but also gradually closes down the possibility of developing an autonomous mechanism for producing the technological innovations that would liberate the potentialities for an indigenous technical structure of production. Moreover, because increments in productivity and therefore in personal income of the workers are linked to technological advances made in other countries, the workers tend to perceive dependency as necessary to their personal betterment. This idea is generally reinforced by the alien culture that is diffused through mass media. In this way the effects of alien—and alienating—technology are propagated through the productive process to social classes, culture, and society.

Dependency is thus revealed as a particular form of relationship between advanced dominant capitalist centers and peripheral dependent capitalist economies. The foregoing analysis of this relationship was made from the standpoint of dependent countries.

[1] Adicea Castillo, "EL sector agrícola y el desarrollo económico," mimeographed (Caracas: Facultad de Ciencias Económicas y Sociales, UCV, January, 1969), p. 6.
[2] Frank Bonilla, *The Failure of the Elites.*
[3] Celso Furtado, *Subdesenvoivimento e estagnação na América Latina* (Rio de Janeiro: Civilização Brasileira, 1968), chap. 2.
[4] Cited by Héctor Silva Michelena, "Neocolonialismo y universidad," unpublished manuscript, p. 14.

Critical Thinking Questions

1. What does the author mean by the term "import-substitution" (or "import-substituting")?

2. One might argue that the United States and Canada too, since they were once European colonies, might be expected to conform to Silva Michelena's "dependency" model. Yet clearly they do not. How does the author address this issue?

3. Which paragraph do you feel best sums up the essence of the article overall. Justify your answer.

Genocide in Rwanda
(1994)

During a period of little more than three months in the spring and early summer of 1994 Rwanda's ethnic Hutus initiated and carried out the massacre of as many as 800,000 of the country's Tutsis. The following account describes some of the circumstances.

It took exactly fifty years . . . *it* or something very like *it* has indeed happened again. Just as Hitler's grand plan was founded on an ingrained European anti-Semitism which he played on by singling out the Jews as the source of all Germany's ills, the Hutu radicals are inheritors of the colonial lunacy of classifying and grading different ethnic groups in a racial hierarchy. While the Jews were described by Nazis as "vermin," the Tutsis were called *invenzi* ("the cockroaches that have to be crushed"). Anti-Tutsi propaganda presented them as a "minority, well-off and foreign"—so similar to the image developed to stigmatize the Jews—and thus an ideal scapegoat for all Rwanda's problems.

. . . [L]ocal media, particularly the radio, play an essential role. . . . [T]he programs in Kinyarwanda broadcast unceasing messages of hate, such as "the grave is only half full. Who will help us fill it?" . . .

On 6 April 1994 the plane carrying President Habyarimana [of Rwanda] and President Cyprien of Burundi was shot down. . . . [This] acted as the fuse for the eruption of violence which led to the greatest tragedy in the history of the country. . . . [Hutu] militia leaders divided up the territory under their control so that one man was allocated for every ten households in order to systematically search for Tutsis. . . . In this way every Tutsi family could be denounced by somebody who knew the members personally: pupils were killed by their teachers, shop owners by their customers, neighbor killed neighbor. . . . Churches where Tutsis sought sanctuary were . . . the scene of some of the worst massacres: 2,800 people in Kibungo, 6,000 in Cyahinda, 4,000 in Kibeho, to give just a few examples. . . . Radio . . . encouraged the violence with statements such as that made at the end of April 1994: "By 5 May, the country must be completely cleansed of Tutsis. . . . The children must be killed too."

The genocide spread rapidly to cover the whole country. . . . By the end of April, it was estimated that 100,000 people had been killed. There are aspects of this genocide which are new and contemporary; others we have seen before. The use of propaganda, the way control was exercised over the administration: these are all reflections of the modern era. So too are the extreme racist ideology and the radical determination to exterminate all Tutsis in one all-encompassing blow. . . . [T]he killings were . . . meticulously well organized. However, the means used to accomplish them were primitive in the extreme: for example, the use of machetes and *unfunis* (wooden clubs studded with metal spikes).

From *Rwanda and Genocide in the Twentieth Century,* translated by Alison Marschner (New York University Press, 1995).

Critical Thinking Questions

1. What are the names of the two African groups cited in the document? Which is represented as the aggressor and which as the victim?

2. Does the author draw any parallels to prior genocides? How does he argue they are similar?

3. Where does the author of the piece appear to lay the blame for the massacres? Explain.

Osama bin Laden, "Hypocrisy Rears Its Ugly Head"
(2001)

The following is a translation of remarks attributed to Osama bin Laden and aired by the al-Jazeera news network about four weeks after the September 11, 2001, terrorist attacks in New York City, Washington, and Pennsylvania.

I bear witness that there is no God but Allah and that Muhammad is his messenger.

There is America, hit by God in one of its softest spots. Its greatest buildings were destroyed, thank God for that. There is America, full of fear from its north to its south, from its west to its east. Thank God for that.

What America is tasting now is something insignificant compared to what we have tasted for scores of years. Our nation [the Islamic world] has been tasting this humiliation and this degradation for more than 80 years. Its sons are killed, its blood is shed, its sanctuaries are attacked, and no one hears and no one heeds.

When God blessed one of the groups of Islam, vanguards of Islam, they destroyed America. I pray to God to elevate their status and bless them.

Millions of innocent children are being killed as I speak. They are being killed in Iraq without committing any sins, and we don't hear condemnation or a *fatwa* [religious decree] from the rulers. In these days, Israeli tanks infest Palestine—in Jenin, Ramallah, Rafah, Beit Jalla and other places in the land of Islam—and we don't hear anyone raising his voice or moving a limb.

When the sword comes down [on America], after 80 years, hypocrisy rears its ugly head. They deplore and they lament for those killers, who have abused the blood, honor and sanctuaries of Muslims. The least that can be said about those people is that they are debauched. They have followed injustice. They supported the butcher over the victim, the oppressor over the innocent child. May God show them his wrath and give them what they deserve.

I say that the situation is clear and obvious. After this event, after the senior officials have spoken in America, starting with the head of infidels worldwide, Bush, and those with him. They have come out in force with their men and have turned even the countries that belong to Islam to this treachery, and they want to wag their tail at God, to fight Islam, to suppress people in the name of terrorism.

When people at the ends of the earth, Japan, were killed by their hundreds of thousands, young and old, it was not considered a war crime, it is something that has justification. Millions of children in Iraq is something that has justification. But when they lose dozens of people in Nairobi and Dar es Salaam [capitals of Kenya and Tanzania, where U.S. embassies were bombed in 1998], Iraq was struck and Afghanistan was struck. Hypocrisy stood in force behind the head of infidels worldwide, behind the cowards of this age, America and those who are with it.

Translation of Osama bin Laden remarks aired by al Jazeera news shortly after September 11, 2001.

These events have divided the whole world into two sides—the side of believers and the side of infidels. May God keep you away from them. Every Muslim has to rush to make his religion victorious. The winds of faith have come. The winds of change have come to eradicate oppression from the island of Muhammad, peace be upon him.

To America, I say only a few words to it and its people. I swear by God, who has elevated the skies without pillars, neither America nor the people who live in it will dream of security before we live it in Palestine, and not before all the infidel armies leave the land of Muhammad, peace be upon him.

God is great, may pride be with Islam. May peace and God's mercy be upon you.

Critical Thinking Questions

1. What is the "hypocrisy" the text refers to?

2. According to the document, what actions will the United States have to take in order to enjoy "security?"

The American Civil Rights Movement

Martin Luther King Jr., Letter from Birmingham Jail (1963)

Dwight D. Eisenhower, Events in Little Rock, Arkansas (1957)

Martin Luther King Jr., Letter from Birmingham Jail
(1963)

King, a Baptist minister in Montgomery, Alabama, successfully adapted the passive resistance techniques of Thoreau and Gandhi to the American civil rights movement. Following his arrest in 1963 for leading a demonstration in Birmingham, Alabama, King was criticized by a group of white clergymen who objected to his methods. The following letter is King's response.

You deplore the demonstrations taking place in Birmingham. But your statement, I am sorry to say, fails to express a similar concern for the conditions that brought about the demonstrations. I am sure that none of you would want to rest content with the superficial kind of social analysis that deals merely with effects and does not grapple with underlying causes. It is unfortunate that demonstrations are taking place in Birmingham, but it is even more unfortunate that the city's white power structure left the Negro community with no alternative.

In any nonviolent campaign there are four basic steps: collection of the facts to determine whether injustices exist; negotiation; self-purification; and direct action. We have gone through all these steps in Birmingham. There can be no gainsaying the fact that racial injustice engulfs this community. Birmingham is probably the most thoroughly segregated city in the United States. Its ugly record of brutality is widely known. Negroes have experienced grossly unjust treatment in the courts. There have been more unsolved bombings of Negro homes and churches in Birmingham than in any other city in the nation. These are the hard, brutal facts of the case. On the basis of these conditions, Negro leaders sought to negotiate with the city fathers. But the latter consistently refused to engage in good-faith negotiation....

We have waited for more than 340 years for our constitutional and God-given rights. The nations of Asia and Africa are moving with jetlike speed toward gaining political independence, but we still creep at horse-and-buggy pace toward gaining a cup of coffee at a lunch counter. Perhaps it is easy for those who have never felt the stinging darts of segregation to say, "Wait". But when you have seen vicious mobs lynch your mothers and fathers at will and drown your sisters and brothers at whim; when you have seen hate-filled policemen curse, kick and even kill your black brothers and sisters; when you see the vast majority of your twenty million Negro brothers smothering in an airtight cage of poverty in the midst of an affluent society; when you suddenly find your tongue twisted and your speech stammering as you seek to explain to your six-year-old daughter why she can't go to the public amusement park that has just been advertised on television, and see tears welling up in her eyes when she is told that Funtown is closed to colored children, and see ominous clouds

---

Reprinted by arrangement with the Estate of Martin Luther King Jr., c/o Writers House as agent for the proprietor New York, NY. Copyright 1963 Dr. Martin Luther King Jr., copyright renewed 1991 Coretta Scott King.

of inferiority beginning to form in her little mental sky, and see her beginning to distort her personality by developing an unconscious bitterness toward white people; when you have to concoct an answer for a five-year-old son who is asking: "Daddy, why do white people treat colored people so mean?"; when you take a cross-country drive and find it necessary to sleep night after night in the uncomfortable corners of your automobile because no motel will accept you; when you are humiliated day in and day out by nagging signs reading "white" and "colored"; when your first name becomes "nigger," your middle name becomes "boy" (however old you are) and your last name becomes "John," and your wife and mother are never given the respected title "Mrs."; when you are harried by day and haunted by night by the fact that you are a Negro, living constantly at tiptoe stance, never quite knowing what to expect next, and are plagued with inner fears and outer resentments; when you are forever fighting a degenerating sense of "nobodiness"—then you will understand why we find it difficult to wait. There comes a time when the cup of endurance runs over, and men are no longer willing to be plunged into the abyss of despair. I hope, sirs, you can understand our legitimate and unavoidable impatience.

You express a great deal of anxiety over our willingness to break laws. This is certainly a legitimate concern. Since we so diligently urge people to obey the Supreme Court's decision of 1954 outlawing segregation in the public schools, at first glance it may seem rather paradoxical for us consciously to break laws. One may well ask: "How can you advocate breaking some laws and obeying others?" The answer lies in the fact that there are two types of laws: just and unjust. I would be the first to advocate obeying just laws. One has not only a legal but a moral responsibility to obey just laws. Conversely, one has a moral responsibility to disobey unjust laws. I would agree with St. Augustine that "an unjust law is no law at all." . . .

I hope you are able to see the distinction I am trying to point out. In no sense do I advocate evading or defying the law, as would the rabid segregationist. That would lead to anarchy. One who breaks an unjust law must do so openly, lovingly, and with a willingness to accept the penalty. I submit that an individual who breaks a law that conscience tells him is unjust, and who willingly accepts the penalty of imprisonment in order to arouse the conscience of the community over its injustice, is in reality expressing the highest respect for law. . . .

I must make two honest confessions to you, my Christian and Jewish brothers. First, I must confess that over the past few years I have been gravely disappointed with the white moderate. I have almost reached the regrettable conclusion that the Negro's great stumbling block in his stride toward freedom is not the White Citizen's Counciler or the Ku Klux Klanner, but the white moderate, who is more devoted to "order" than to justice; who prefers a negative peace which is the absence of tension to a positive peace which is the presence of justice; who constantly says: "I agree with you in the goal you seek, but I cannot agree with your methods of direct action"; who paternalistically believes he can set the timetable for another man's freedom; who lives by a mythical concept of time and who constantly advises the Negro to wait for a "more convenient season."

Shallow understanding from people of good will is more frustrating than absolute misunderstanding from people of ill will. Lukewarm acceptance is much more bewildering than outright rejection. . . .

You speak of our activity in Birmingham as extreme. At first I was rather disappointed that fellow clergymen would see my nonviolent efforts as those of an extremist. I began thinking about the fact that I stand in the middle of two opposing forces in the Negro community. One is a force of complacency, made up in part of Negroes who, as a result of long years of oppression, are so drained of self-respect and a sense of "somebodiness" that they have adjusted to segregation; and in part of a few middle-class Negroes who, because of a degree of academic and economic security and because in some ways they profit by segregation, have become insensitive to the problems of the masses. The other force is one of bitterness and hatred, and it comes perilously close to advocating violence. It is expressed in the various black nationalist groups that are springing up across the nation, the largest and best-known being Elijah Muhammad's Muslim movement. Nourished by the Negro's frustration over the continued existence of racial discrimination, this movement is made up of people who have lost faith in America, who have absolutely repudiated Christianity, and who have concluded that the white man is an incorrigible "devil."

I have tried to stand between these two forces, saying that we need emulate neither the "do-nothingism" of the complacent nor the hatred and despair of the black nationalist. For there is the more excellent way of love and nonviolent protest. I am grateful to God that, through the influence of the Negro church, the way of nonviolence became an integral part of our struggle....

... Perhaps the South, the nation and the world are in dire need of creative extremists.

I had hoped that the white moderate would see this need. Perhaps I was too optimistic; perhaps I expected too much. I suppose I should have realized that few members of the oppressor race can understand the deep groans and passionate yearnings of the oppressed race, and still fewer have the vision to see that injustice must be rooted out by strong, persistent and determined action. I am thankful, however, that some of our white brothers in the South have grasped the meaning of this social revolution and committed themselves to it....

Critical Thinking Questions

1. What can be learned or inferred from the document about the nature of the criticisms King is responding to?

2. How does King justify his methods, which are sometimes contrary to the law?

3. Summarize the essence of King's response in your own words.

Dwight D. Eisenhower, Events in Little Rock, Arkansas
(1957)

Little Rock's school district began in the summer of 1957 to implement desegregation, but was undermined by the state governor, Orville Faubus, who worried about his chances for reelection should integration go ahead. A complicated confrontation soon developed as at first the National Guard, then white mobs, acted to keep African-American students from attending Central High School. President Eisenhower eventually intervened, sending in the military to reestablish order.

My Fellow Citizens. . . . I must speak to you about the serious situation that has arisen in Little Rock. . . . In that city, under the leadership of demogogic extremists, disorderly mobs have deliberately prevented the carrying out of proper orders from a federal court. Local authorities have not eliminated that violent opposition and, under the law, I yesterday issued a proclamation calling upon the mob to disperse.

This morning the mob again gathered in front of the Central High School of Little Rock, obviously for the purpose of again preventing the carrying out of the court's order relating to the admission of Negro children to that school.

Whenever normal agencies prove inadequate to the task and it becomes necessary for the executive branch of the federal government to use its powers and authority to uphold federal courts, the President's responsibility is inescapable.

In accordance with that responsibility, I have today issued an Executive Order directing the use of troops under federal authority to aid in the execution of federal law at Little Rock, Arkansas. This became necessary when my Proclamation of yesterday was not observed, and the obstruction of justice still continues. It is important that the reasons for my action be understood by all our citizens.

As you know, the Supreme Court of the United States has decided that separate public educational facilities for the races are inherently unequal and therefore compulsory school segregation laws are unconstitutional. . . .

During the past several years, many communities in our southern states have instituted public school plans for gradual progress in the enrollment and attendance of school children of all races in order to bring themselves into compliance with the law of the land.

They thus demonstrated to the world that we are a nation in which laws, not men, are supreme. I regret to say that this truth—the cornerstone of our liberties—was not observed in this instance. . . .

Here is the sequence of events in the development of the Little Rock school case. In May of 1955, the Little Rock School Board approved a moderate plan for the gradual desegregation of the public schools in that city. It provided that a start toward

---

From Public Papers of the Presidents of the United States: Dwight D. Eisenhower, 1957.

integration would be made at the present term in the high school, and that the plan would be in full operation by 1963.... Now this Little Rock plan was challenged in the courts by some who believed that the period of time as proposed in the plan was too long.

The United States Court at Little Rock, which has supervisory responsibility under the law for the plan of desegregation in the public schools, dismissed the challenge, thus approving a gradual rather than an abrupt change from the existing system. The court found that the school board had acted in good faith in planning for a public school system free from racial discrimination.

Since that time, the court has on three separate occasions issued orders directing that the plan be carried out. All persons were instructed to refrain from interfering with the efforts of the school board to comply with the law.

Proper and sensible observance of the law then demanded the respectful obedience which the nation has a right to expect from all its people. This, unfortunately, has not been the case at Little Rock. Certain misguided persons, many of them imported into Little Rock by agitators, have insisted upon defying the law and have sought to bring it into disrepute. The orders of the court have thus been frustrated.

The very basis of our individual rights and freedoms rests upon the certainty that the President and the Executive Branch of Government will support and insure the carrying out of the decisions of the federal courts, even, when necessary, with all the means at the President's command....

Mob rule cannot be allowed to override the decisions of our courts.

Now, let me make it very clear that federal troops are not being used to relieve local and state authorities of their primary duty to preserve the peace and order of the community....

The proper use of the powers of the Executive Branch to enforce the orders of a federal court is limited to extraordinary and compelling circumstances. Manifestly, such an extreme situation has been created in Little Rock. This challenge must be met and with such measures as will preserve to the people as a whole their lawfully protected rights in a climate permitting their free and fair exercise.

The overwhelming majority of our people in every section of the country are united in their respect for observance of the law—even in those cases where they may disagree with that law.... A foundation of our American way of life is our national respect for law.

In the South, as elsewhere, citizens are keenly aware of the tremendous disservice that has been done to the people of Arkansas in the eyes of the nation, and that has been done to the nation in the eyes of the world.

At a time when we face grave situations abroad because of the hatred that communism bears toward a system of government based on human rights, it would be difficult to exaggerate the harm that is being done to the prestige and influence, and indeed to the safety, of our nation and the world.

Our enemies are gloating over this incident and using it everywhere to misrepresent our whole nation. We are portrayed as a violator of those standards of conduct which the peoples of the world united to proclaim in the Charter of the United Nations. There they affirmed "faith in fundamental human rights" and "in the dignity and worth of the human person" and they did so "without distinction as to race, sex, language or religion."

And so, with deep confidence, I call upon the citizens of the State of Arkansas to assist in bringing to an immediate end all interference with the law and its processes. If resistance to the federal court orders ceases at once, the further presence of federal troops will be unnecessary and the City of Little Rock will return to its normal habits of peace and order and a blot upon the fair name and high honor of our nation in the world will be removed.

Thus will be restored the image of America and of all its parts as one nation, indivisible, with liberty and justice for all.

Critical Thinking Questions

1. What appeared to be Eisenhower's primary motivation for sending in the military?

2. Are any other motivations than the one you noted in the previous answer apparent? Briefly explain.

V. Map Exercises

Map Exercises

The Americas

Europe

Africa & the Middle East

Asia & the South Pacific

Placenames for Map Quiz: the Americas

*Major cities and geographic features are located on regional, geographic maps.

Countries & Cities

Countries

Haiti	Canada	Jamaica
Guatemala	Paraguay	Brazil
United States	Honduras	Chile
Argentina	Venezuela	Uruguay
Surinam	Peru	Costa Rica
Mexico	Dominican Republic	Ecuador
Panama	El Salvador	Bolivia
Guyana	Cuba	Columbia
French Guiana	Nicaragua	

Selected Capital Cities

Santiago	Lima	Bogotá
Mexico City (Tenochtitlán)	Buenos Aires	Caracas
Havana	Quito	

Major Cities*

Vera Cruz	Recife
Rio de Janiero	Cuzco

Geographic Features*

Continents & Regions

North America	Central America	South America

Rivers & Bodies of Water

Arctic Ocean	Caribbean Sea	Amazon River
Pacific Ocean	Gulf of Mexico	Mississippi River
Atlantic Ocean	Strait of Magellan	

Peninsulas

Yucatan Peninsula

Land Features (Not Labeled)

Andes Mountains	Atacama Desert

North America: Countries

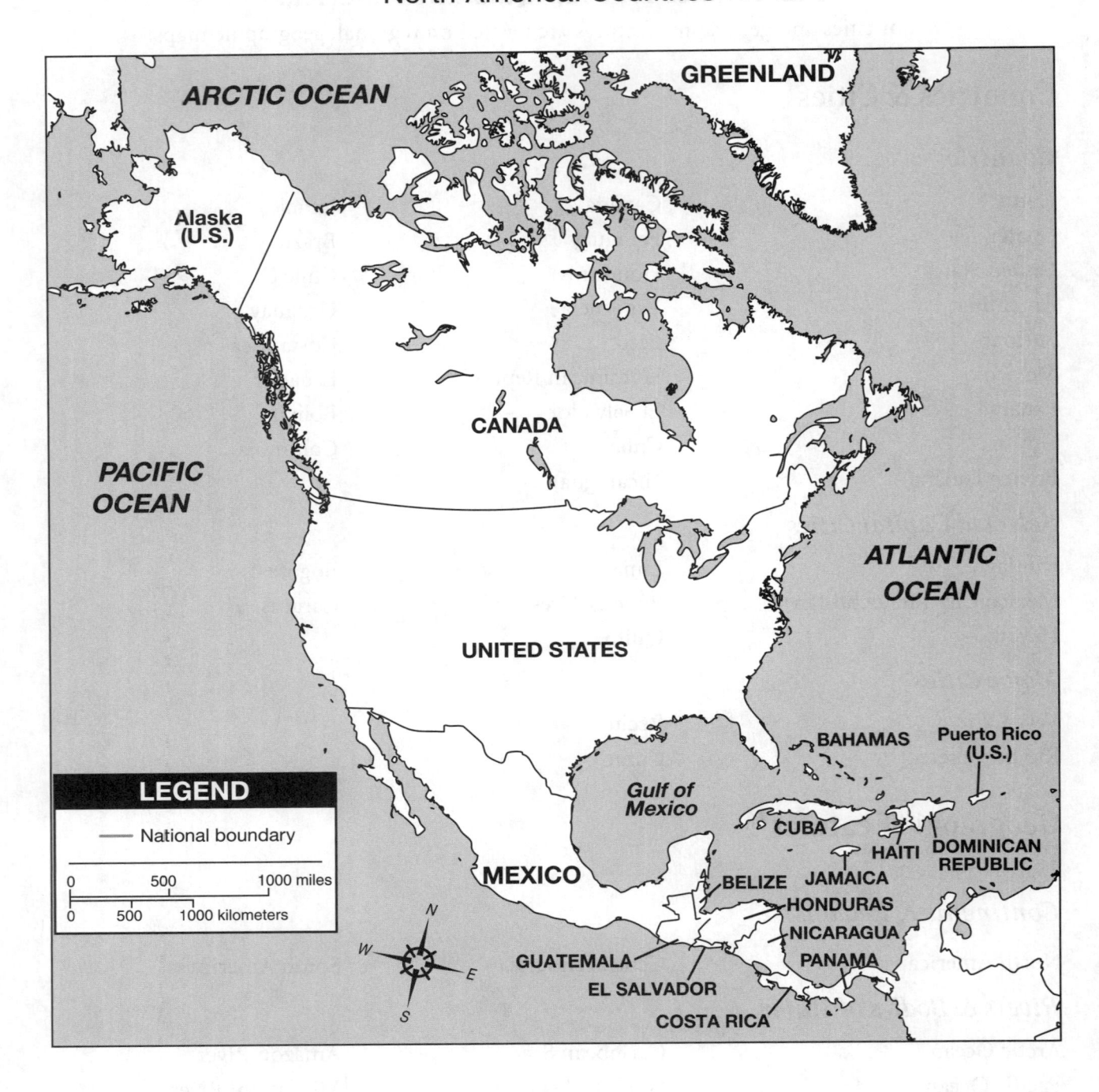

North America: Countries

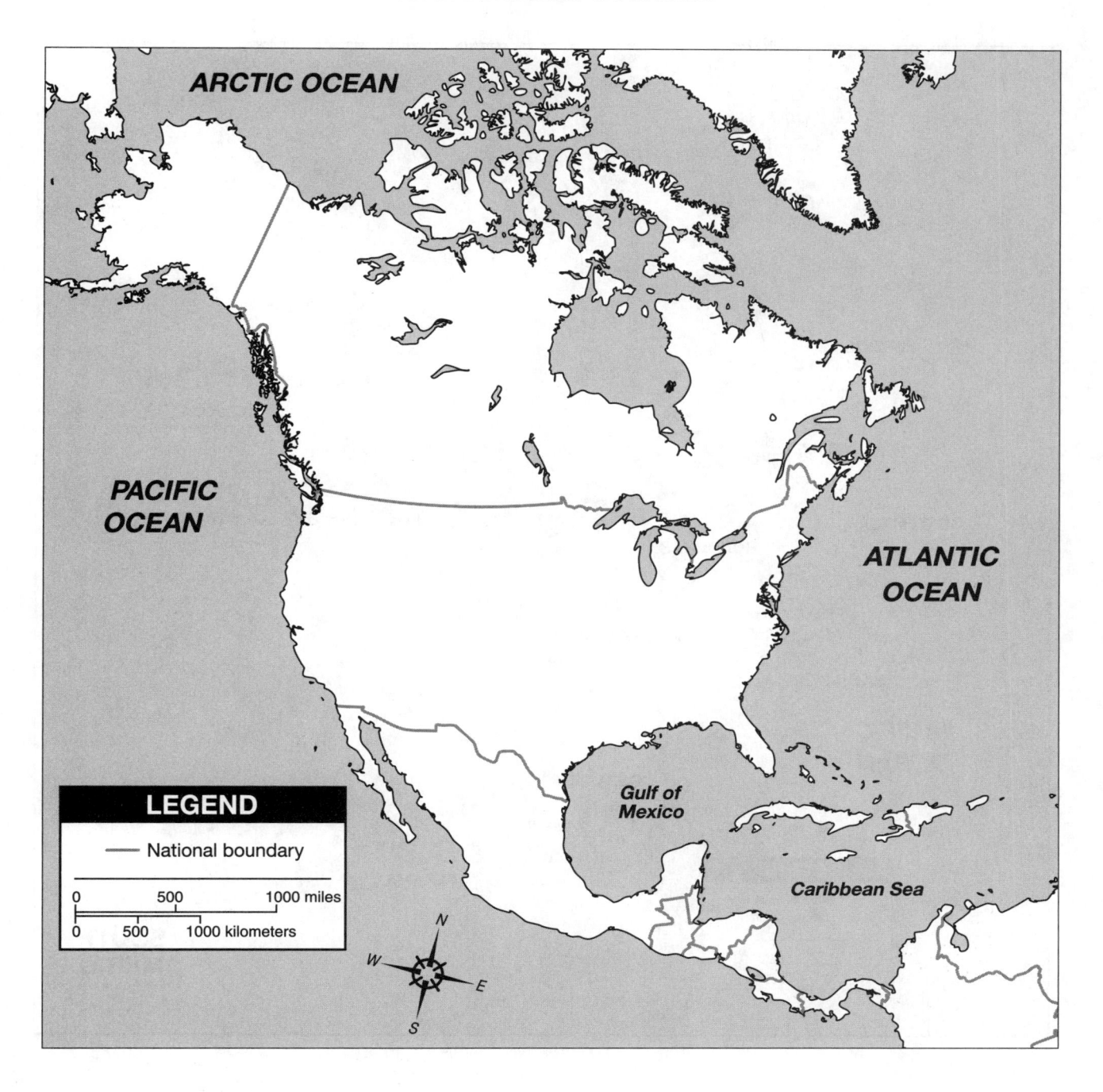

ARCTIC OCEAN

PACIFIC OCEAN

ATLANTIC OCEAN

Gulf of Mexico

Caribbean Sea

LEGEND
— National boundary

0 500 1000 miles
0 500 1000 kilometers

N W E S

175

Central America: Political

Central America: Political

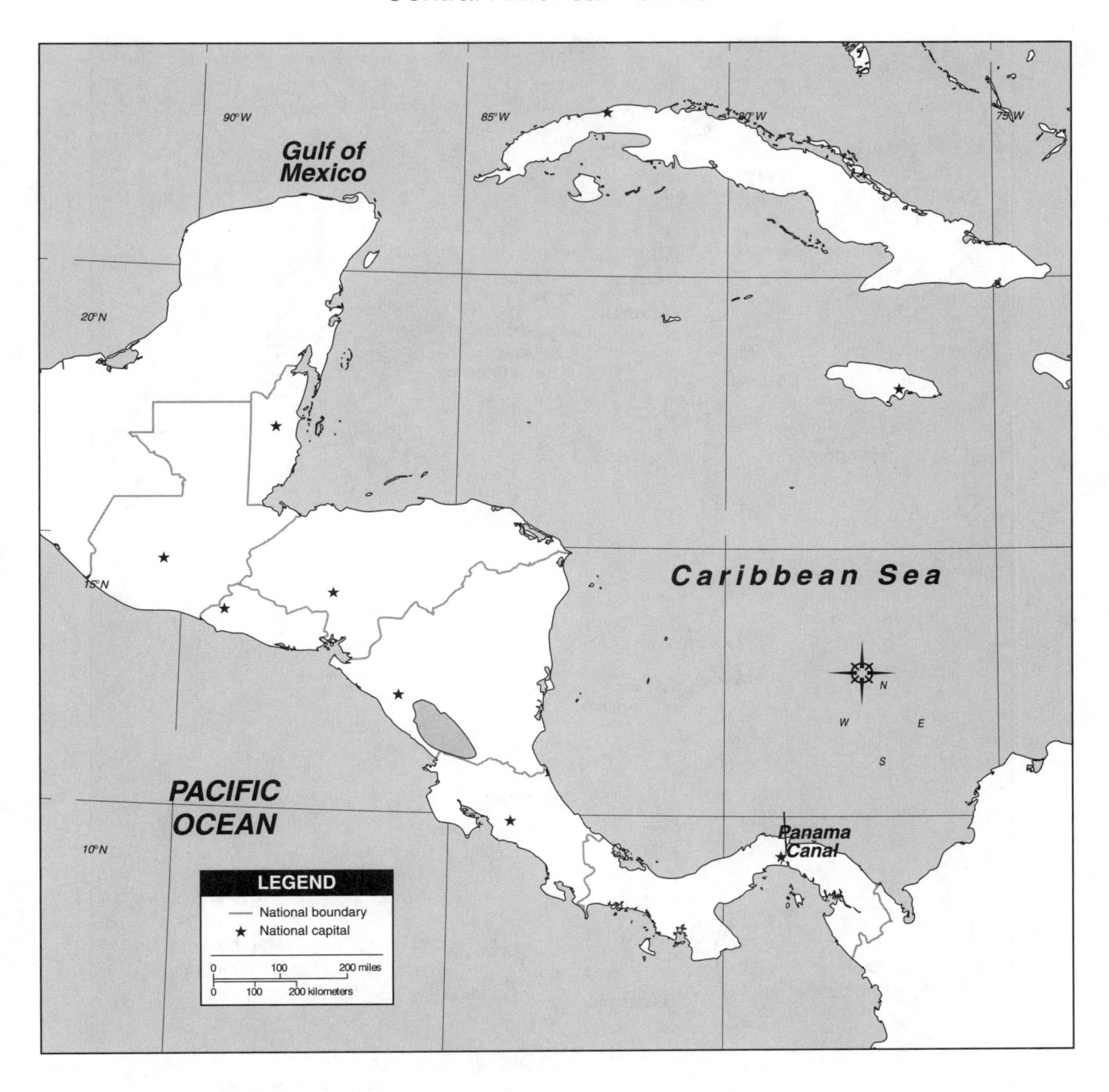

South America: Political

South America: Political

Americas: Geographic Features

Americas: Geographic Features

Placenames for Map Quiz: Europe

*Geographic features are located on regional, geographic maps.

Countries & Cities

Countries

Italy	Ukraine	Belgium
Netherlands (Holland)	Ireland	Portugal
France	Spain	Slovakia
Albania	Luxemburg	Denmark
Germany	Sweden	Poland
Switzerland	Norway	Bulgaria
Austria	Yugoslavia	Greece
Hungary	Romania	Czech Republic
Finland	Latvia	Lithuania
Estonia	Russia	Bosnia
Belarus	Slovenia	Macedonia
Croatia	Great Britain (UK)	

Selected Capital Cities

London	Lisbon	Copenhagen
Paris	Vienna	Sarajevo
Rome	Moscow	Berlin
Madrid	Amsterdam	

Geographic Features*

Continents & Regions

Europe

Rivers & Bodies of Water

Mediterranean Sea	Strait of Gibraltar	Don River
Black Sea	English Channel	Vistula River
Baltic Sea	Danube River	Elbe River
Caspian Sea	Volga River	Dnieper River
North Sea	Rhine River	Tagus River
Aegean Sea	Loire River	

Peninsulas & Islands

Iberian Peninsula	Corsica	Sardinia
Crimean Peninsula	Sicily	Crete
Balkan Peninsula	Cyprus	

Land Features (Not Labeled)

Caucasus Mountains	Pyrenees Mountains
Carpathian Mountains	Alps Mountains

European Countries

European Countries

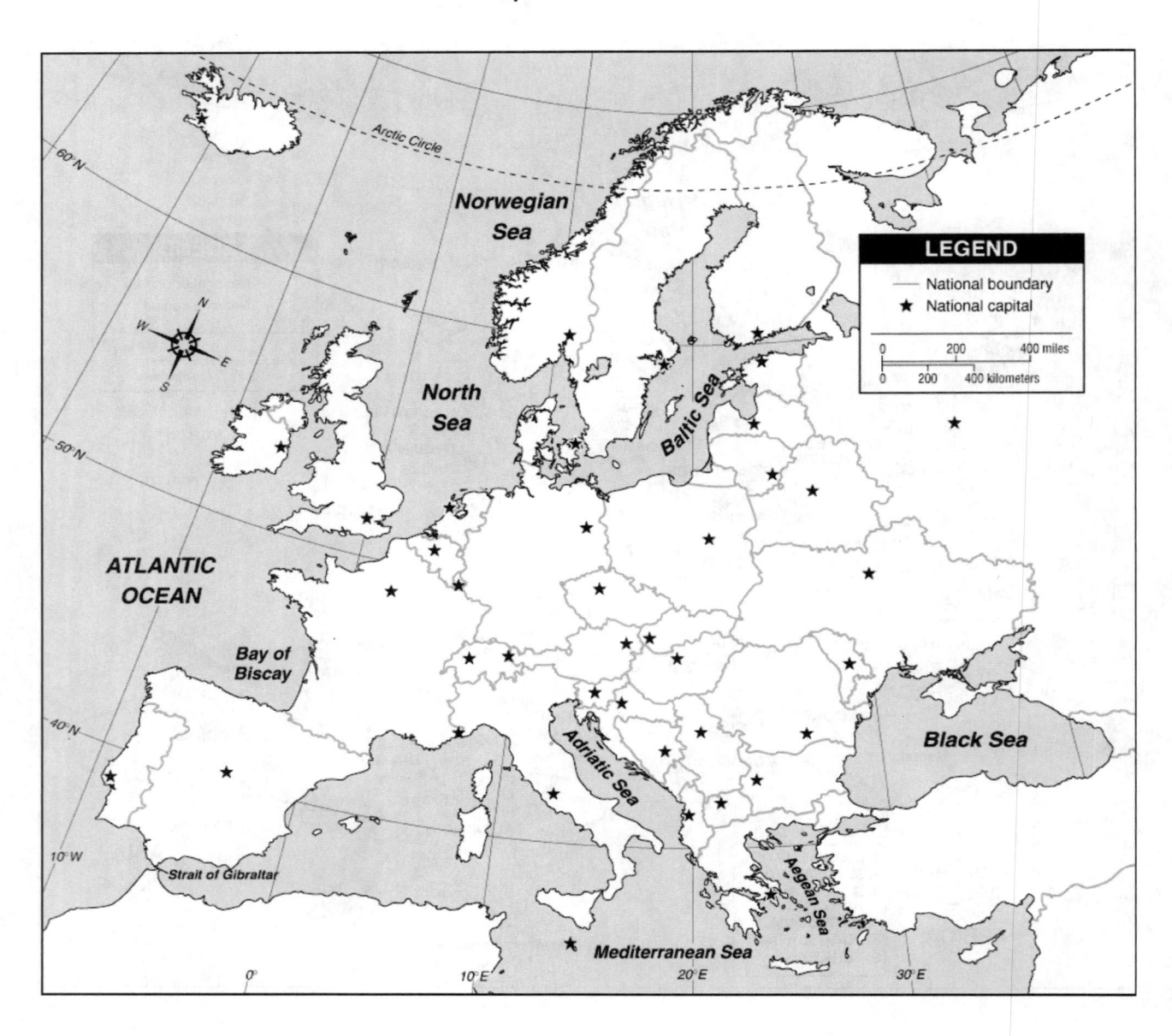

Europe: Geographic Features

Europe: Geographic Features

Placenames for Map Quiz: Africa

*Major cities and geographic features are located on regional, geographic maps.

Countries & Cities

Countries

Ethiopia	Namibia	Nigeria
Niger	South Africa	Morocco
Libya	Madagascar	Guinea
Algeria	Liberia	Ghana
Mali	Togo	Gabon
Mauritania	Malawi	Zambia
Central African Republic	Egypt	Botswana
Angola	Chad	Zimbabwe
Uganda	Somalia	Burkino Faso
Senegal	Kenya	Sierre Leone
Tunisia	Congo Republic	Benin
Ivory Coast	Mozambique	Democratic Republic of Congo
Cameroon	Tanzania	Sudan

Selected Capital Cities

Cairo	Kigali	Khartoum
Nairobi	Mogadishu	Tunis

Major Cities*

Timbuktu	Mombassa	Cape Town

Geographic Features*

Continents & Regions

Africa

Rivers & Bodies of Water

Nile River	Congo River	Niger River

Land Features (Not Labeled)

Sahara Desert	Kalahari Desert

Placenames for Map Quiz: the Middle East/Southwest Asia

*Major cities and geographic features are located on regional, geographic maps.

Countries & Cities

Countries

Turkey	Iraq	Israel
Jordan	Saudi Arabia	Lebanon
Kuwait	Oman	Iran (Persia)
Syria	Yemen	

Selected Capital Cities

Tehran	Damascus	Tel Aviv
Baghdad	Ankara	Beirut

Major Cities*

Mecca   Jerusalem

Geographic Features*

Continents & Regions

the Middle East

Rivers & Bodies of Water

Red Sea   Persian Gulf

Africa and Southwest Asia: Political

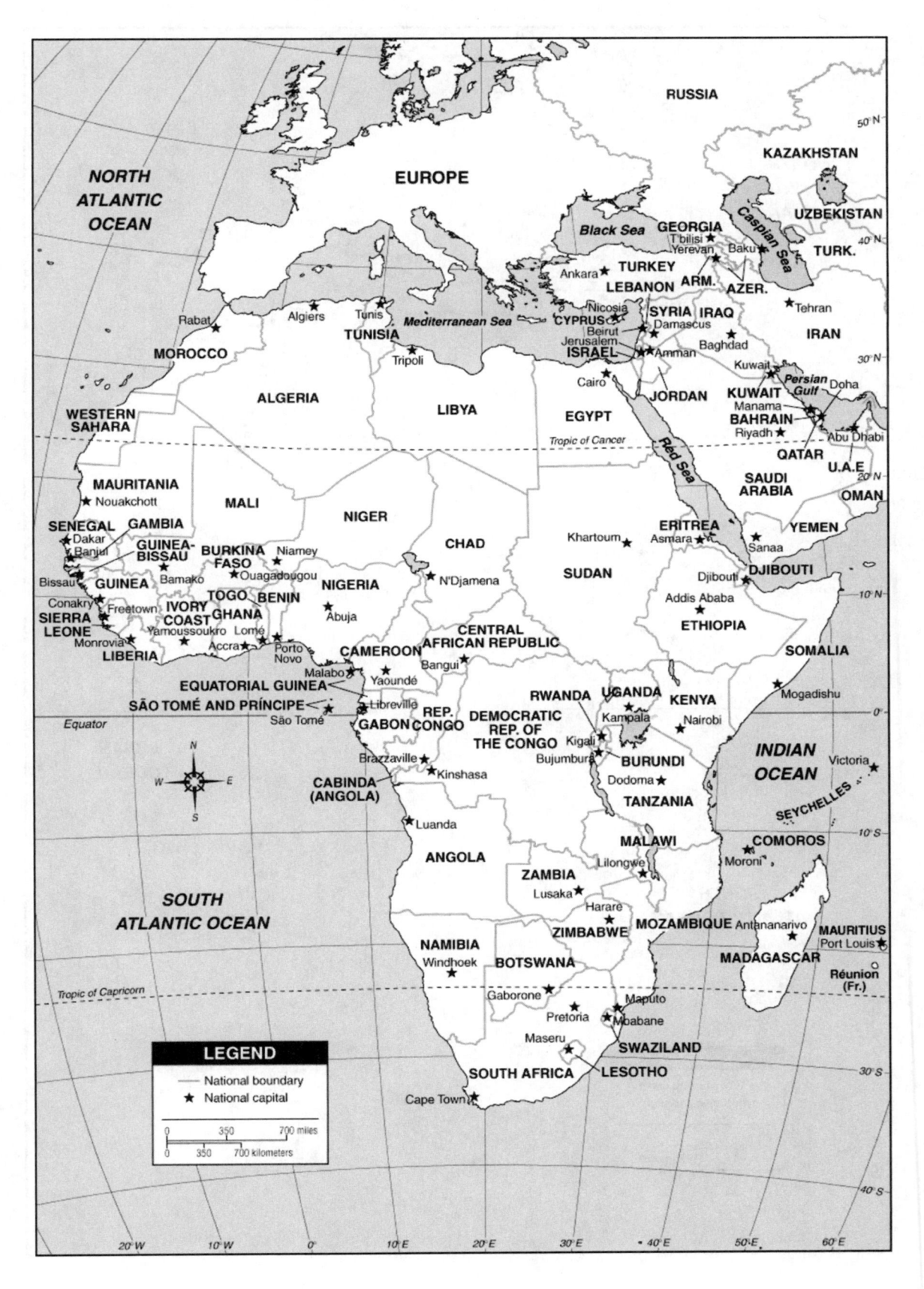

Africa and Southwest Asia: Political

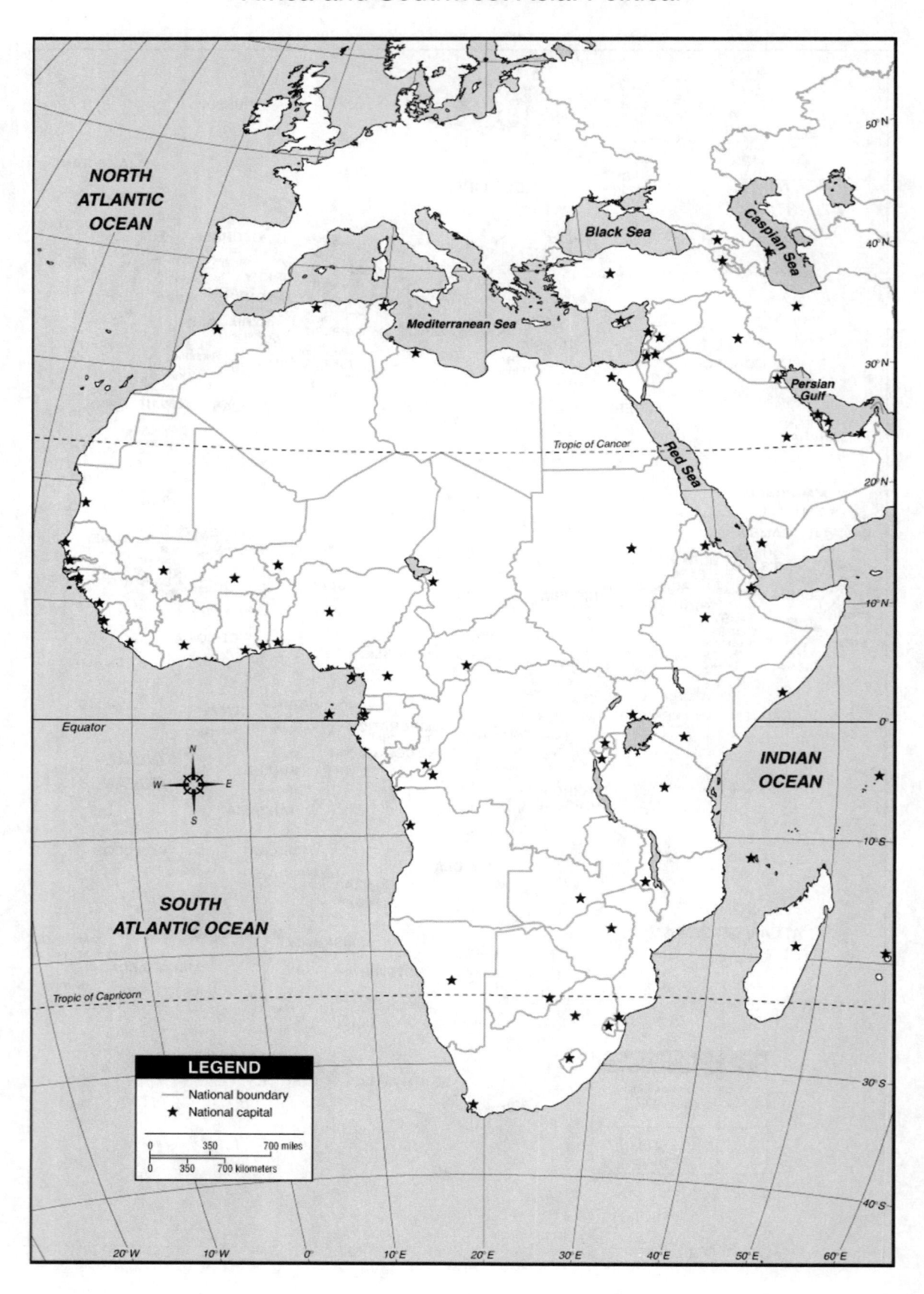

Africa & the Middle East: Geographic Features

191

Africa & the Middle East: Geographic Features

Placenames for Map Quiz: Asia & the South Pacific

*Major cities and geographic features are located on regional, geographic maps.

Countries & Cities

Countries

Kazakhstan	Georgia	Uzbekistan
Kyrghyzstan	Turkmenistan	Afghanistan
India	Tadzhikstan	China
Malaysia	Pakistan	Laos
Thailand	Nepal	Bangladesh
Mongolia	Sri Lanka (Ceylon)	Burma
Indonesia	Vietnam	Taiwan
South Korea	Japan	Azerbaijan
North Korea	Philippines	
Cambodia	Armenia	

Selected Capital Cities

New Delhi	Tokyo	Bangkok
Hanoi	Beijing (Peking)	Manila
Phnom Penh	Kabul	

Major Cities*

Calcutta	Shanghai	Guangzhou (Canton)
Mombai (Bombay)	Hong Kong	Ho Chi Minh City (Saigon)

Geographic Features*

Continents & Regions

Asia	India	Australia

Rivers & Bodies of Water

Indian Ocean	Indus River	Yangtze (Chang) River
China Sea	Ganges River	Mekong River
Bay of Bengal	Yellow (Huang) River	

Islands

Sumatra	Borneo

Land Features (Not Labeled)

Himalaya Mountains	Ural Mountains	Gobi Desert

Asia and the South Pacific: Political

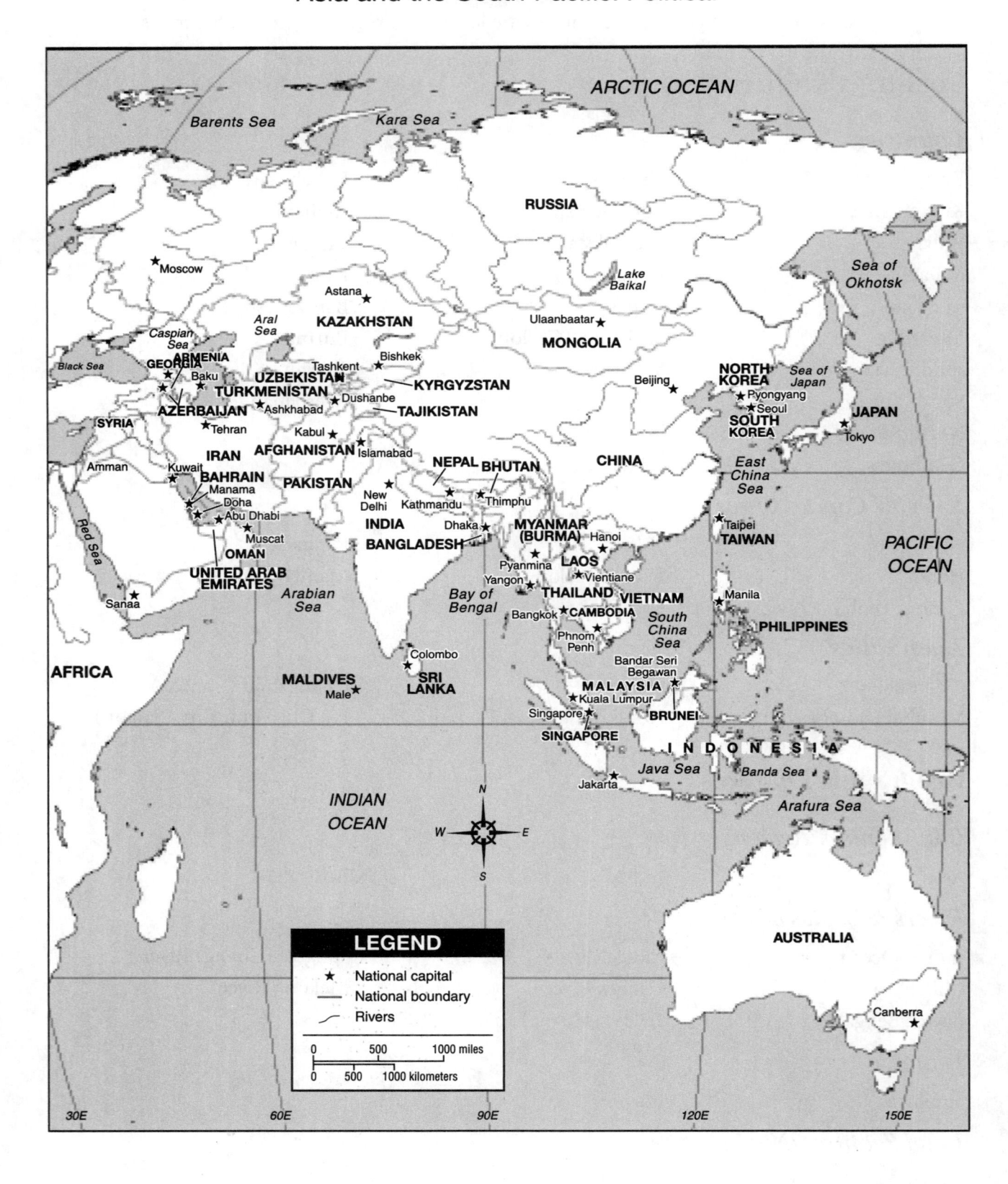

Asia and the South Pacific: Political

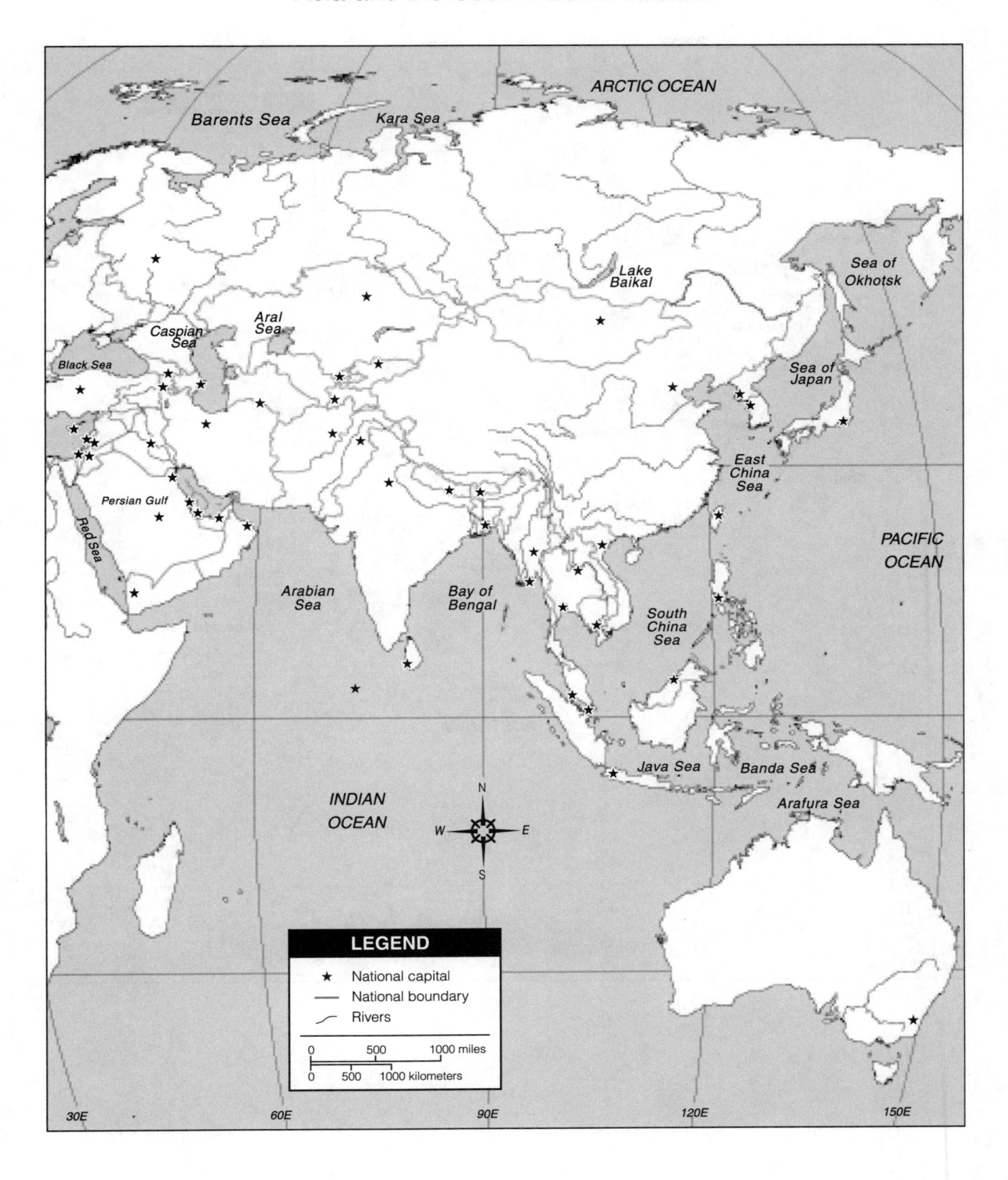

LEGEND
- ★ National capital
- — National boundary
- ⌒ Rivers

Southeast Asia and the South Pacific: Political

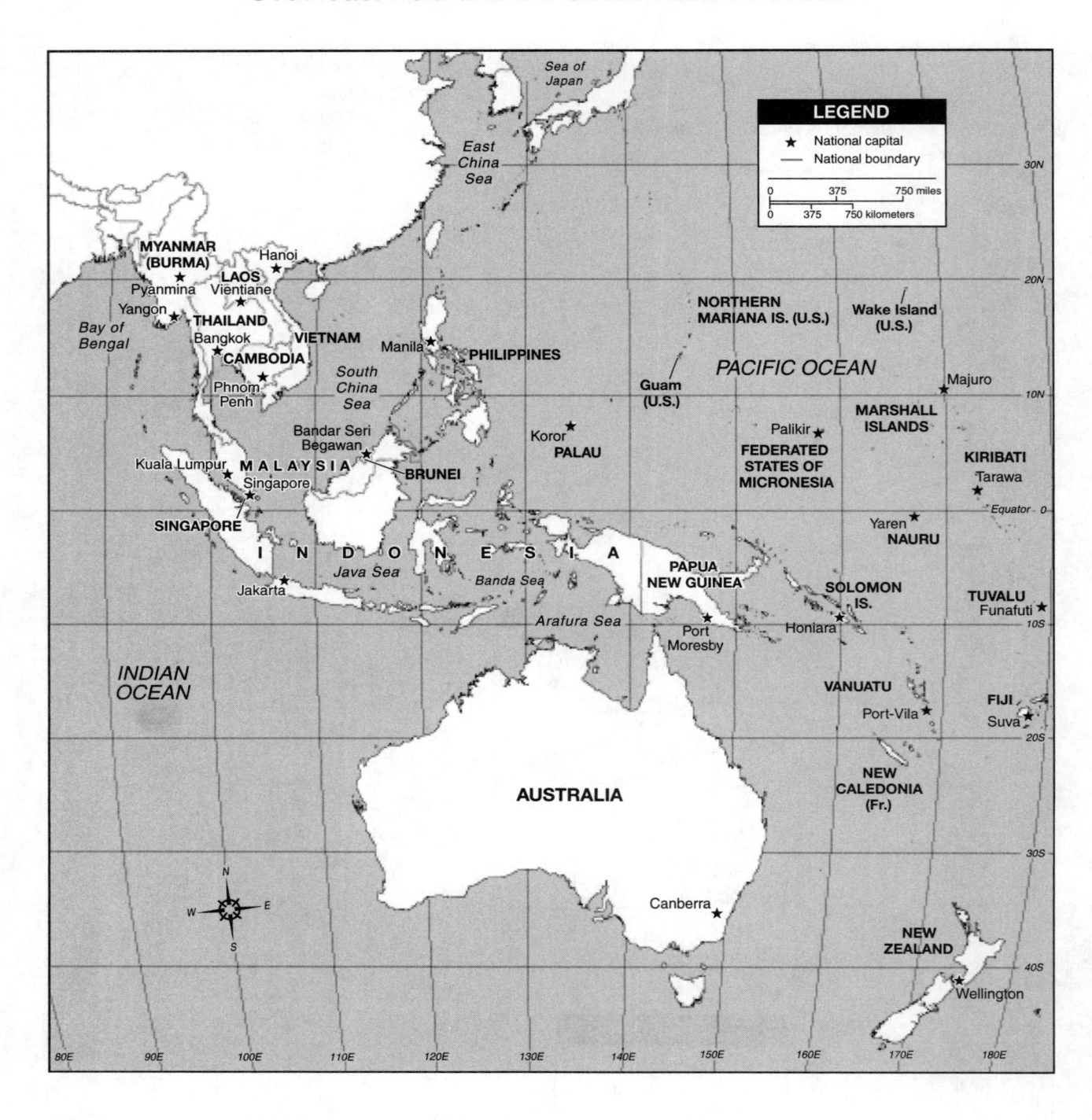

Southeast Asia and the South Pacific: Political

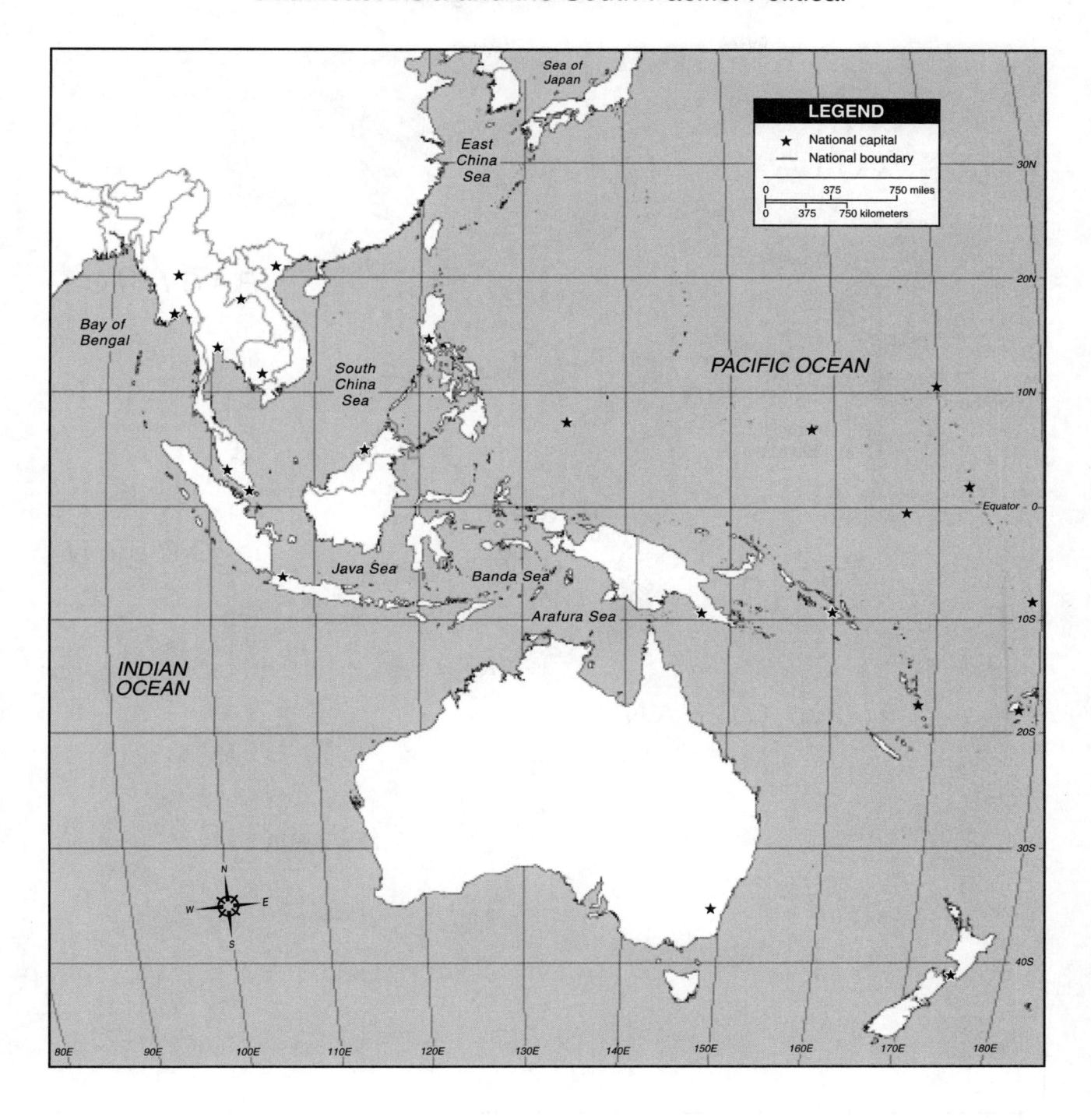

Asia & the South Pacific: Geographic Features

Asia & the South Pacific: Geographic Features